The Moral Mind

Henry Haslam

SOCIETAS

essays in political
& cultural criticism

imprint-academic.com

Published in the UK by Societas
Imprint Academic, PO Box 200, Exeter EX5 5YX, UK

Published in the USA by Societas
Imprint Academic, Philosophy Documentation Center
PO Box 7147, Charlottesville, VA 22906-7147, USA

ISBN 184540 016 X
A CIP catalogue record for this book is available from the
British Library and US Library of Congress

*

Cover photograph

Imperfect reflection:
Suilven reflected in the waters of Loch Inver, Scottish Highlands

Contents

Preface

Morality lies at the meeting point of several disciplines. Moral philosophy, theology, psychology, neuroscience, evolutionary biology and studies of animal behaviour all have their contributions to make. And, since the subject matter is the human personality, ideas from other sources can also add to the greater picture. Where there has been a gap in the literature, a gap that this volume attempts to fill, is a simple review of moral thinking, illustrating its wide diversity. As a result, general statements are made about morality without really considering just what morality is. For example, some writers claim that morality is consistent with the principle of natural selection, while others maintain that it is wholly at variance with it. There is an element of truth in both statements: it all depends on which aspects of morality you choose to look at. In this book I have set out to review a wide range of moral sentiments so that we can then see how far the evidence supports ideas such as these. The topics covered range from temptation to guilt, from altruism to fairness, from sex to economics, from forgiveness to animal welfare, and from cruelty in nature to the future of the planet.

The main part of this book, therefore, consists of a survey of the moral mind, looking at various different kinds of moral sentiment. As I brought together my accounts of different topics, I found that they naturally grouped themselves under three headings: the morality of instinct, the morality of custom, and the morality of beyond. This, rather tentative, attempt at classification helps to illustrate the diversity of our moral sentiments.

The moral sense is deeply embedded in the human mind, and it is possible to describe it without making any assumptions about how it connects with religious belief. Many people today recognise the need for a system of moral values that believers (I am a Christian myself) and non-believers can share, and the starting point is to examine and try to understand the range of moral sentiments and values that we hold.

Acknowledgements I received a great deal of helpful advice from Helen Oppenheimer, who reviewed the book, and from Anthony Freeman at Imprint Academic. Jeremy Harvey, Michael Haslam, Jean Kelly and Jane Plant also read the book in draft and gave me their comments. I am grateful to them all.

Henry Haslam
Taunton, August 2005

Chapter 1

Introduction

> I fully subscribe to the judgement of those writers who maintain that of all the differences between man and the lower animals, the moral sense or conscience is by far the most important.
>
> Charles Darwin, *The Descent of Man*

The moral mind is an important part of what it is to be human. Our sense of right and wrong is deeply rooted in human nature. It is not easy to define, but we know that it exists. It comes naturally to us to consider that we, or other people, ought or ought not to have acted in a certain way, and it matters to us.

The moral sense is one of the characteristics that set us apart from other animals. We have other mental abilities, too, that are uniquely human, in that we can apply our minds in ways that no other species can. We can think about ourselves and our own mental processes, for example: we are self-conscious. We can focus our minds outside the here-and-now: we can think about what is taking place on the other side of the world, we can think about the past, and we can think about the future. We can hold political debates, and we can talk about yesterday's football. All of these abilities provide us with extra skills and understanding, but the moral sense is different in that it provides us with values, a particular way of looking at the world. Charles Darwin, in the quotation at the head of this page, says that he agrees with the view that the moral sense is the most important of the differences between humans and other animals. He goes on to say that this sense is summed up in the word 'ought'. Recent writers also consider that morality is an important defining attribute of human beings. This is implicit, for example, in the book titles *The Ethical Primate* (by the philosopher Mary Midgley, published in 1994) and *The Moral Animal* (by science writer Robert Wright, also 1994) and in the chapter heading 'The Sanctimonious Animal' in *The Blank Slate* by the psychologist Steven Pinker (2002).

Definitions

Reason and words derived from it have two common meanings. In one sense they refer to a process of logic that gets us from a starting point to a conclusion. If the starting point is false, the conclusion is likely to be false too ('Garbage in, garbage out', as they say about computers). In this sense, reason is a tool, not a motivation, and is only used if there is some incentive to do so, even if the incentive is no more than a love of reasoning. This is the sense that Hume (1739/40) was using when he wrote 'Reason is, and ought only to be the slave of the passions, and can never pretend to any other office than to serve and obey them.' Reason is also used in a very different sense, meaning intuitive good sense, combined with consideration for other people. When we talk about 'a reasonable person' or 'unreasonable behaviour', we are not talking about cold logic; we are referring to general good sense and a willingness to accommodate to other people (or a lack of these). Modern writers who argue for a system of morality based on reason probably include both meanings of the word: they are pleading for intuitive good sense as the basis, combined with a willingness to listen to other people's opinions, and also for principles that are open to discussion by logical argument.

Emotions or *feelings* (equivalent to Hume's 'passions' in the passage just quoted) provide the driving force for reasoning, as well as for behaviour in general.

Instincts are innate, inherited patterns of thought and behaviour in humans and other animals. They can be powerful motivating forces. *Custom* refers to a generally accepted way of behaving that is specific to a particular society, acquired by learning from other individuals and therefore not passed on genetically. Instinctive behaviour and customs are both shared behaviours (i.e. not restricted to single individuals); the former are habits that are passed on genetically, while the latter are habits that are learned from others.

Continued on page 4

The view that no other species has a moral sense is supported by two of the greatest twentieth-century observers of animal behaviour, Konrad Lorenz, who studied numerous species, wild and tame, and Jane Goodall, whose career was devoted to a study of our closest relatives, chimpanzees, in their natural habitat in Tanzania. To read the work of these dedicated and meticulous observers is to realise how similar human behaviour is to that of other animals, in so many ways; it is therefore particularly significant that both of them should emphasise that humans are unique in their sense of right and wrong.

Konrad Lorenz, in *Man Meets Dog* (1954), writes, 'For a wild animal in its natural state, there is no conflict between natural inclinations and what they "ought" to do, and this is the paradise which man has lost'. Further on, he writes, 'True morality, in the highest human sense of the word, presupposes a mental capacity which no animal possesses'. In *On Aggression* (1966), he writes at some length about 'behavioural analogies to morality' — implying that, however similar their behaviour might be, other animals are not motivated by moral thinking or moral considerations.

Jane Goodall wrote *Through a Window* (1990) after spending 30 years studying the chimpanzees of Gombe. She described numerous similarities in the way that chimpanzees and humans behave. The studies that led to the recognition of so many similarities also served to highlight those aspects in which humans are unique — differences, above all, in intellectual abilities. This intellectual ability gives us a greater depth of understanding. Thus, only we 'are capable of real cruelty — the deliberate infliction of physical or mental pain on living creatures despite, or even because of, our precise understanding of the suffering involved. ... Only we, surely, are capable of evil.' On the other hand, 'we should remember that we alone among the life forms of this planet are able to overcome, by conscious choice, the dictates of our biological natures.'

Why should we make that conscious choice? Why don't we go along with the dictates of our biological natures? Other species get along very well by simply following their natural impulses. They live according to patterns of behaviour that work. Some individuals display aberrant behaviour, but most individuals, most of the time, seem to have no difficulty in following normal patterns of behaviour. Natural selection will ensure that any aberrant behaviour that severely reduces the prospects for survival will not become the normal behaviour of the species. Why aren't humans like that? How did they come to acquire this special attribute, the moral sense?

Definitions
(*continued from page 2*)

Conscience and *moral sense* both refer to the inner voice that makes moral judgements; conscience is more subjective, relating to our own behaviour ('My conscience is telling me to …'; 'I have a guilty conscience about …'). The moral sense is more detached and objective: it makes judgements on general issues and other people's behaviour, as well as our own. The words *good*, *bad*, *kind* and *cruel*, used in a moral context to describe behaviour, express a moral judgement on the behaviour in question.

Altruism (in humans) is a concern for the well-being of others. Altruistic behaviour (in humans and other animals) is behaviour that benefits another at some cost to the altruist. There is normally no expectation of any benefit in return (for the concept of 'reciprocal altruism' see page 44). Altruism and selfishness are discussed on pages 27 and 40 respectively.

Natural selection (page 32) is the evolutionary process described by Charles Darwin by which random mutations of genetic material produce variants of a species, and those variants which are best able to survive in the environment in which they live are those that prosper and have offspring inheriting similar characteristics. It has an important role in the *evolution* of life forms, but it is not the only means by which evolution takes place.

The word *sociobiology* was coined by E O Wilson (1975), who defined it as the systematic study of the biological basis of all social behaviour; great importance was attached to natural selection. The related term *evolutionary psychology* is variously defined; expressed simply, it is the attempt to understand the human mind in an evolutionary perspective.

The term *moral principle* is used for any general principle like truth-telling or kindness. Different moral principles sometimes come into conflict, and one will have to defer to the other (as truth-telling sometimes gives way to kindness).

Recent studies of chimpanzees and other primates, notably by Frans de Waal and his colleagues (e.g. 1989, 1996, 2001; Flack and de Waal, 2000), have sought to show how the moral sense can be understood in an evolutionary context. Primates show many of the kind of responses to social situations which, in humans, would be described as morally good, such as caring for the young (their own and others), conflict resolution and repayment of kindnesses, but de Waal and his colleagues recognise that humans are the only truly moral beings.

During the course of the book we shall look in more detail at some of the differences, as well as similarities, between humans and other animals. We shall see how far evolutionary theory and our animal ancestry help us to understand our moral behaviour and thinking, and we shall also see how close other animals come to the possession of a moral sense.

A study of the moral mind

In considering morality and the moral sense, it is important to keep in mind the distinction between four separate (but interrelated) issues:

(1) Objective morality. The question of whether absolute, objective moral values exist or whether morality is entirely a matter of personal opinion has been much debated. For people with a religious faith, God is the author and authority of absolute moral values, but belief in the reality of objective moral values is not confined to religious believers. Some of the arguments for and against the existence of objective moral values are set out in Chapter 2.

(2) The moral sense. The human mind has a sense of right and wrong. We can ask moral questions, make moral judgements and strive to understand objective morality. Just as we all have our own, unique personality, so we have our own unique (and, to that extent, subjective) view of what is right and wrong. Our moral values develop during the course of our lives, and they are, at best, an imperfect reflection of absolute moral values. A study of the various ways in which the moral sense is expressed in the human personality forms the central part of this book.

(3) Good and bad behaviour. The moral sense enables us to apply the words 'good' or 'bad' to certain ways of behaving, but the behaviour itself exists independently of our moral judgement — and behaviour that we might describe as good or bad existed in nature long before there were any humans around

to understand moral concepts, experience moral sentiments, make moral judgements and be motivated by moral considerations.

(4) A moral code: a set of rules based on moral considerations. The term can be used for the personal rules that one person tries to live by, or for the rules that a society lays down for its members to obey. The book looks at the thinking underlying moral rules, but it does not set out to discuss moral codes themselves.

The word 'morality' can be used to cover any or all of these concepts, and there is often no need to distinguish between them — like when we say 'It is wrong to steal.' It is when trying to analyse or explain morality or account for its origin that it is essential to be clear exactly what it is that we are discussing.

The activities of humans and animals (3) are facts, which can be observed and recorded, and so is a moral code (4), if clearly defined. Moral feelings and sentiments (2) are also facts. To be precise, the fact that they exist is 'a scientific fact like any other', whereas the moral sentiments that they express may or may not be objective truth but represent the 'fundamental data' of ethics (Russell, 1954). Attempts to explain or account for these facts are hypotheses. Opinions as to whether an objective morality (1) exists are also hypotheses.

Humans and other animals often perform good deeds (3) for reasons that are unrelated to any moral considerations; people with a strong moral sense often succumb to temptation and perform bad deeds, contrary to the guidance of their moral sense; and people acting in obedience to their moral sense have been known to do things and to hold opinions that most readers of this book would describe as 'bad' (in meting out punishment for wrongdoing, for example). Thus, if we behave well, it does not follow that we were influenced by moral considerations. If we behave badly, it does not follow that we gave no thought to moral considerations. If we are agreed about the importance of leading a moral life, it does not follow that we will agree about what kinds of behaviour are and are not morally good. When we describe humans as the only moral animals, therefore, we are not saying that they behave better than other animals. What we are saying is that humans are the only animals capable of moral judgement. We are the only animals for whom moral concepts such as 'good', 'bad', 'temptation', 'guilt' and 'ought' have meaning.

Moral living involves choice. We make a judgement that one course of action is morally better than another. Where choice exists, the result is not a foregone conclusion: if morality is real, temptation and wrongdoing are also realities (see page 37).

Ethics has hitherto been largely the preserve of philosophers and theologians, not of psychologists or other scientists. Different disciplines have their own contributions to make. Moral philosophers are concerned with good behaviour, and try to establish systems that can form the basis of moral thinking. Philosophers also examine processes of thought, using reasoning, logic and analysis. Theologians seek to establish what is and is not good behaviour, based on learning to understand the will of God.

Several writers have advocated a greater role for science in the study of morality and moral behaviour, including Lorenz (1966), Wilson (1975), Hinde (2002) and Gazzaniga (2005). One of the ways that scientific enquiries work is to collect information first, recording observations about the natural world, and then see what conclusions can be drawn from the observations. This is where there seems to be a gap in the literature about moral thinking, a gap which this book attempts to fill.

Chapter 2 of the book provides a background to the study and includes summaries of aspects of moral philosophy that are relevant to the theme of the book. The central part of the book, Chapter 3, is a survey of moral thinking, looking at the moral sense itself and at ways in which it interacts with the complicated mixture of mental processes that together make up human nature: it reinforces many of the patterns of thought and behaviour that we have inherited from our pre-human primate ancestors ('The morality of instinct'); it leads us to obey — or to challenge — the customs of our own people ('The morality of custom'); and it leads us beyond these conventions to broaden our sympathies, our understanding and our vision as we seek a different, uniquely human way of thinking about our place in the world ('The morality of beyond'). Chapter 4 considers some of the conclusions that can be drawn from the survey and suggests how we may be able to work towards a new consensus on moral issues.

Chapter 2

Setting the Scene

2-1. The Denial of Moral Values

Since we are moral beings to the core, any theory of human behaviour that does not take morality 100 per cent seriously is bound to fall by the wayside.

Frans de Waal, *Good Natured*

For most of history, it would have been taken for granted that morality was important and that the word 'ought' had meaning. Great thinkers have considered what was good and bad behaviour, and many volumes have been written on the subject. However, for a large part of the twentieth century, much of what had previously been taken for granted was questioned. New philosophical approaches, combined with the decline of religious belief, left many people confused about the value and validity of moral sentiments. Many decent, honest, caring people became uncomfortable with the idea of moral scruple, fearful that such scruples may not be intellectually defensible, and yet equally uncomfortable with a world view that has no place for the moral dimension.

In a world of liberal values and expanding horizons, when we were learning to appreciate the worth of people and societies who did things differently to ourselves, we were no longer satisfied with a traditional system of values in which everything was clear cut. There was a general feeling that tolerance, understanding and compassion were more important than strict adherence to traditional moral codes. Tolerance, understanding and compassion are, of course, also moral virtues, and, as Mary Midgley (1991) points out, many of the objections to the practice of making moral judgements are, in fact, *moral* objections. However, the word 'morality' was apt to be associated with rigid codes of the past which many people wanted to overthrow anyway.

James Q Wilson wrote in 1993 at the start of his book *The Moral Sense*, 'Virtue has acquired a bad name', and he went on to suggest that some of us have 'tried to talk ourselves out of' having a moral sense. Simon Blackburn, in *Being Good* (2001), wrote, 'What bothers [people], I believe, are the many causes we have to fear that ethical claims are a kind of sham.' It became smart to be cynical, to deride moral sentiments and to take it for granted that all human behaviour was influenced by base motives.

The purpose of this chapter is to argue that morality is worth taking seriously and that the moral sense is a valid subject for study. The first part considers some of the philosophical ideas that have led us to question the validity of morality as a subject worth studying (the approaches known as logical positivism, emotivism, moral relativism, and the argument from queerness) and at their widespread influence. The belief that moral thinking can be disregarded as a motive force in human behaviour may have had its origin in philosophy, but it has spread more widely and may be seen in psychology and sociology (pages 18–21) and even in economics (page 21).

Philosophy

Logical positivism and emotivism

Of the many philosophers who have questioned the validity of moral statements, A J ('Freddie') Ayer was one of the most influential. He was a leading adherent of the logical positivist school of philosophy, which held that a statement is only meaningful if, in principle, it is possible to prove that it is true or false. Since moral statements cannot be proved or disproved, they were dismissed as having no factual basis and therefore being of no interest (to philosophers of the logical-positivist school, that is). In a famous passage in his first and most important book, *Language, Truth and Logic*, published in 1936, Ayer wrote:

> The presence of an ethical symbol in a proposition adds nothing to its factual content. Thus if I say to someone, 'You acted wrongly in stealing that money,' I am not stating anything more than if I had simply said, 'You stole that money.' In adding that this action is wrong I am not making any further statement about it.

He went on to say that the statement 'Stealing money is wrong' has no factual meaning: it is simply an expression of moral sentiment or emotion (his view is therefore known as the 'emotivist' theory of morality). It follows, from this view, that if two people disagree about some moral issue, there is no sense in asking which of them is right, since neither is asserting a genuine proposition.

Ayer's emotivist view of moral thinking was the dominant philosophical view in the English-speaking world after the second world war. It was not only to philosophers and academics that his views were communicated, however. He was a brilliant performer on television, and this enabled his ideas to reach a wide audience through his appearances on *The Brains Trust*, where he expounded his view that the sense of morality was of no interest because it was not subject to proof.

The 'logic' of logical positivism could lead, though, to conclusions that were contrary to our inner convictions. Bertrand Russell, one of the outstanding intellects of the twentieth century, was not unsympathetic to the ways of the logical positivists; it is also clear from his life and his writings that he was a man of powerful moral convictions. In 1960 he wrote:

> I cannot see how to refute arguments for the subjectivity of moral values, but I find myself incapable of believing that all that is wrong with wanton cruelty is that I don't like it.

He found that the evidence of his own inner convictions was at odds with the theoretical 'arguments' that moral values are entirely subjective. His convictions told him one thing: theory told him another. The history of science and my own personal experience as a scientist lead me to the view that when theoretical arguments are at odds with the facts (and, as we have seen, Russell himself (1954) pointed out that the fact that we have moral emotions 'is a scientific fact like any other'), one should pay attention to the facts and wait for new discoveries or new insights that will enable a better theory to be developed.

Moral relativism

Another twentieth-century philosopher, J L Mackie, introduced the first chapter of his book *Ethics: inventing right and wrong* (1977) with the bald statement, 'There are no objective values.' He went on to say that there were two main arguments in support of this thesis, the argument from relativity and the argument from queerness.

The argument from relativity has been around for a long time and, indeed, it contains a great deal of truth. It is easy to see that different societies have different moral codes in some matters, just as they have different patterns of conventional behaviour. In the modern world we have learned to accept the social conventions of other societies with less disapproval than in the past. Provided that we restrict the term 'moral' to the kind of traditional moral precepts which vary from one society to another and which many people in our society would like to discard anyway, it may be quite easy to regard moral standards as no different from other social conventions and to contend, with Mackie, that the moral code merely reflects conventional behaviour.

However, not all moral sentiments can be treated so lightly. Let us take eating habits as an example, since they vary so much between one society and another. Some differences may be regarded as interesting (whether you drink tea from a bowl or a cup, for example). Other customs may be regarded as weird and perhaps distasteful (such as eating animals and animal parts that are not part of your own customary diet), and others as barbaric (thoughtlessly inflicting unnecessary pain on animals, perhaps). But what about cannibalism? How easily can the moral relativist regard killing other human beings for food as being as acceptable as any other eating habit?

Opponents of the argument from relativity point out that, although there are large variations in specific moral codes, there are some general principles which are shared by them all, like kindness, generosity, fairness and honesty (e.g. Lewis, 1943, 1952; Taylor, 2004). Mackie refutes this by arguing that strong moral sentiments tend to be attached to specific issues (of the kind that vary from one community to another) rather than to generalised principles:

> That is, people judge that some things are good or right, and others are bad or wrong, not because — or at any rate not only because — they exemplify some general principle for which widespread implicit acceptance could be claimed, but because something about those things arouses certain responses immediately in them, though they would arouse radically and irresolvably different responses in others. 'Moral sense' or 'intuition' is an initially more plausible description of what supplies many of our basic moral judgements than 'reason'.

The fundamental weakness of the relativist argument is the same as that of the emotivist argument: that people think that their moral sentiments are more than just personal opinions or a reflection of social customs and shared attitudes. The strongest reason for believing that the term 'good behaviour' has some objective meaning is that we are convinced that this is the case. One thing we can all agree about is that our strongest moral convictions relate to something outside ourselves, beyond our own personal feelings. We do not, most of us, claim that we have a perfect understanding of what constitutes absolute, objective morality, but we do feel that objective morality exists and that our own sentiments represent a reaching out towards it. When we express our moral convictions we are appealing to something outside ourselves, something that we expect other people to recognise. People who have strong views on either side of the abortion issue (the woman's right to have an abortion, or the foetus's right to life), for example, are likely to be appealing to some authority outside themselves; they are unlikely to consider their opponents' viewpoint as being just as valid as their own. A statement like 'It is always good to betray your family and friends' offends against what we know to be true just as much as an assertion that a square table is round. Almost everybody has some moral convictions that seem to be more than just personal opinions. If you disagree with somebody's moral values, you may try to produce evidence or reasons why the specific values under dispute are false, but you do not try to argue that the underlying premise, namely that moral values exist, is false. Indeed, the more strongly you dispute your opponent's moral values, the more firmly committed you are to the belief that an objective morality exists. When we talk about the 'moral high ground', we don't just mean a bump on the brain.

Could we be mistaken in our sense that objective morality exists? Certainly, people can be deluded in their beliefs, and we often are, but our delusions are generally personal to ourselves, and there is generally evidence, visible to ourselves or to other people, that we are deluded. In contrast, the belief that our moral values relate to something outside ourselves is common to everyone who possesses a moral sense, and there is no evidence that can persuade us to doubt it.

In fact, it has been seriously suggested that a belief in an objective morality is just that: a collective illusion, put together by our genes in order to make us function better (Ruse and Wilson, 1986). The idea that a collective illusion could be created by evolutionary processes is curious, and does seem to invite criticism:

(1) Howard Taylor (2004) and Philip Rolnick (2004) point out that if the delusion is good for us, it must be bad that Ruse and Wilson have disillusioned us. If evolutionarily successful behaviour depends upon our being duped by our genes, it is likely that our behaviour would change when the scales fell from our eyes; those of us who have been disillusioned would become less successful. This argument appears to be supported by Ruse himself (1991): '... if we recognised morality to be no more than an epiphenomenon of our biology, we would cease to believe in it and stop acting upon it'.

(2) Ruse and Wilson recognise that humans believe in the existence of objective morality. They then make the assumption

that moral thinking and moral behaviour (like all behaviour) are favoured by natural selection. This leads them to suggest that the belief in objective moral values is also favoured, because it encourages moral behaviour. Since the belief itself is favoured, they conclude that there is no reason to suppose that objective morality actually exists: an illusory belief would serve the purpose just as well. However, their assumption that moral thinking and moral behaviour are favoured by natural selection is not supported by the evidence (see pages 34–36 and 81–88), and this undermines their reasoning and their conclusion.

(3) If it was our genes that caused the illusion, was it their genes that led Ruse and Wilson to tell the world that morality was an illusion? Mikael Stenmark (2001) points out that, according to their own strict evolutionary theory, the most dominant determinant in scientific behaviour is maximising evolutionary fitness; if they want us to believe their results, they have to tell us that they were motivated not by fitness but by the objective search for truth and understanding — in other words that scientific enquiry is an exception to their evolutionary theory (this theme is discussed at some length by O'Hear, 1997).

If the case for saying that objective morality is an illusion is dismissed, Occam's Razor[1] would lead us to favour the existence of an objective morality that we cannot explain, in preference to a delusion of an objective morality that we cannot explain. It is reasonable to conclude, on present evidence, that objective moral values do exist.

The argument from queerness

Mackie's other argument against objective values (and he considers this argument even more important) is the argument from queerness. 'If there were objective values,' he writes, 'then they would be entities or qualities or relations of a very strange sort, utterly different from anything else in the universe. Correspondingly, if we were aware of them, it would have to be by some special faculty of moral perception or intuition, utterly different from our ordinary ways of knowing everything else.'

Mackie's description, it seems to me, describes objective morality and the moral sense rather well. I sometimes use the term 'moral dimension'. Different dimensions in space are related to one another in such a way that it is possible for an object to move along

---

[1] 'Essentia non sunt multiplicanda praeter necessitatem', or 'Essences are not to be multiplied without necessity'; William of Occam (1290–1349).

one of them without any movement along the others. Each is independent of the others. So it is with moral thinking. Although it interacts with other kinds of mental process (such as reason and emotion), it cannot be controlled by them and it cannot be defined by them. The argument from queerness seems to amount to nothing more than a statement that it is most improbable that such an independent dimension should exist and Mackie is therefore reluctant to accept that it does.

Richard Dawkins, in *The Blind Watchmaker* (1986), has a bit of fun at the expense of Bishop Hugh Montefiore, who found himself unable to accept that natural selection was sufficient to account for all of the complexities of the natural world. The chapters in Montefiore's book *The Probability of God* (1985) dealing with this issue are peppered with phrases like 'It is hard to understand ...' and 'I cannot see how ...' Dawkins counted 16 such examples in one chapter and 35 in another. He dubs this the 'Argument from Personal Incredulity' and says that he considers it to be an extremely weak argument. There is not a lot of difference between the argument from personal incredulity and the argument from queerness. Both can be applied to a theory that seems to be inconsistent with the writer's personal world view and which therefore seems to be very improbable.

Objective morality, to which our moral sense is forever reaching out and which remains beyond our grasp or understanding, is certainly improbable. It would be quite possible to design a universe without it. But improbability has never been enough to stop something existing. What could be more improbable than the elephant's trunk, let us say, or a migrating swallow, or a colony of ants — or, indeed, the human species? Or, indeed, the universe itself? The argument from queerness says no more than that it is most amazing that the moral sense should exist at all. As indeed it is: Immanuel Kant's (1788) sentiments are often quoted:

> Two things fill the mind with ever-increasing wonder and awe, the more often and the more intensely the mind of thought is drawn to them: the starry heavens above me and the moral law within me.

Discussion

The influence on popular twentieth-century thinking of ideas such as those of Ayer and Mackie was immense. They caught the popular mood and appealed to those who wished to overthrow traditional values. Moral cynicism and moral relativism were able to claim an intellectual respectability that they do not deserve. One of the consequences of this was that those who wanted to attach importance to moral considerations were confused and uneasy. They appeared to have the worst of the argument, their sentiments easily derided by a contemporary culture that set no store by moral principles.

Two writers who were so concerned about this prevailing mood, with its denial of values, that they felt moved to protest against it were the English scholar and Christian writer C S Lewis and the lawyer and politician Lord Hailsham. Their books show the power and influence of the prevailing mood.

Lewis's book *The Abolition of Man* was first published in 1943. In it he castigated a little book for schools which had the general effect of undermining and ridiculing a pupil's belief in any kind of values, and he went on to lament the destructive effect such teaching would have on a generation of children and to present a well-argued case for the natural law (the moral law within us, part of our human nature), showing that there is a great deal of agreement on moral values between different traditions throughout the world.

In the early 1990s Lord Hailsham experienced a bout of depression. *Values: Collapse and Cure* is his account of this, written in his own hand and published facsimile in 1994. He attributed his depression to the 'nihilism', as he called it, which he saw all around him, a denial of values. His answer was to emphasise the necessity 'to recognise the objective validity of a natural morality, even though it is incapable of definition'.

Towards the end of the twentieth century, philosophers became more aware of the weaknesses of the relativist and emotivist theories and showed a greater willingness to accept the worth of moral thinking. Here are some selected quotations from philosophers who are willing to consign these views to history: 'long after the demise of Logical Positivism ...' (Thomas Nagel, in *Mortal Questions*, 1979); 'Ayer's book, which may now seem to us brilliant and ingenious, but also unsophisticated and dotty ...' (Iris Murdoch, *Metaphysics as a Guide to Morals*, 1992); 'More generally, emotivism does not fit human experience' (Jenny Teichman and Katherine C Evans, *Philosophy: a beginner's guide*, 1995); 'The aftermath of logical positivism ...' (Mary Warnock, *An Intelligent Person's Guide to Ethics*, 1998); 'Relativism gets a very bad press from most moral philosophers. The "freshman relativist" is a nightmare figure of introductory classes in ethics ...' (Simon Blackburn, *Being Good*, 2001). Around the turn of the century there was a spate of books that took for granted that morality was worth taking seriously and worth writing about.

This tide of philosophical thinking has been slow to reach the general public. It is not only in introductory classes in ethics that relativists are to be found. Unaware of recent trends in philosophy, and wanting to avoid any charge of being judgemental or lacking in compassion, or of being committed to values which they fear cannot be defended against critical attack, they are found throughout society. There are still people who believe that (or fear that) relativism carries weight. For example, two quotations from *The Times* in 2004: '[This] film deserves a generous response at this time of moral relativism'; '… the unstoppable, or at least unstopped, march of relativism.'

As Mary Warnock (1998) wrote, a prevailing cynicism such as this 'may have a creeping and insidious effect, and especially so in schools, where teachers may find themselves bewildered by their own half-articulate principles that they must not be dogmatic, they must not presume that there are any disinterested or unbiased arguments, and above all they must not be "judgemental".' Commendable though it is to avoid being judgemental, if by this we mean unsympathetic condemnation (see page 69), and to show understanding and compassion for those who differ from us, the overall effect has been to leave society rudderless, lacking in values, lacking in any common belief. It has been seen as intellectually untenable to hold firm moral beliefs or to recognise moral thinking as a motive force for human behaviour. To assume that people are not motivated by moral considerations is to demean human nature and is an insult to everyone whose actions have been governed by the wish to act for the best, to behave in a moral way.

It is worth noting that this uneasiness about moral thinking was largely confined to the realm of theory. In practice, in their daily lives, people continued to hold moral convictions and pass judgement on their own actions and those of other people — just as they always have.

We all have our own viewpoints, and we all have our own views. Few of us are so arrogant as to believe that ours are the only true values. We recognise the diversity of moral systems and value systems that exist, but we have a sense that these values connect in some way to something outside ourselves, and it is this 'something' that validates our own personal judgements. It may escape definition, but we know it is there; without it, our personal value judgements are as worthless as the relativists and emotivists would suggest. If we are led to believe that our moral sense is generated entirely within ourselves, in the same way as our gastronomic fads and fancies, for example, we are left bemused and perplexed: something important has been taken away from us. We don't know quite what it is, so we find it difficult to respond.

Difficult to respond, perhaps, in the language of theory, the language of rational argument, the language of logical proof and 'verifiable' statements (Ayer's word). But we *know* that the moral sense differs from other feelings. 'People feel that moral rules are universal. Injunctions against murder and rape, for example, are not matters of taste or fashion but have a transcendent and universal warrant' (Pinker, 2002). 'The basis of morality is a belief that good and harm to particular people (or animals) is good or bad not just from their point of view, but from a more general point of view, which every thinking person can understand' (Nagel, 1987).

The statements 'I want to steal that money' and 'I don't want to steal that money' are opposites. They are also equivalent, in that they both express my state of mind. No one can contradict me. I know whether I have a wish to steal, and that's that. The statements 'I want to steal that money' and 'I ought not to steal that money (even though I won't be caught, no one will know, and the firm, with its multi-million pound turnover, won't be hurt by the loss of £100)' are conflicting statements, but they are not equivalents. They are different in kind. When I say 'I ought not to steal that money' I am engaging with, or appealing to, something outside myself.

When I say 'Apples taste nicer than pears' and you say 'Pears taste nicer than apples', we know that we are each expressing a personal opinion, unconnected with anything outside ourselves. When I say 'We should pay that person back for the harm he has done to us; we ought not to let him get away with it' and you say 'We should forgive him; we ought not to take revenge', we disagree and we are expressing our own points of view, but we are both appealing to principles which extend beyond ourselves, which are 'in some sense there already' (Hare, 1952). We are each, in our own way, seeking to do as we ought.

We each have our own individual sense of right and wrong, but each of us, in our own way, is trying to represent or point to or strive towards some absolute, objective standards of right and wrong. Our personal moral values may be no more than an imperfect reflection of objective values, but we believe that those objective values are real.

This relationship between the subjective and the objective is illustrated by the last lines of Rudyard Kipling's *When Earth's Last Picture is Painted*:

> When Earth's last picture is painted and the tubes are twisted and dried,
> When the oldest colours have faded, and the youngest critic has died,
> We shall rest, and, faith, we shall need it — lie down for an æon or two,
> Till the Master of All Good Workmen shall put us to work anew.

...

And only The Master shall praise us, and only The Master shall blame;
And no one shall work for money, and no one shall work for fame,
But each for the joy of the working, and each, in his separate star,
Shall draw the Thing as he sees It for the God of Things as They are!

In moral thinking, each person expresses 'the Thing as he sees It', But 'the Thing as he sees It' only makes sense if, beyond, there exist 'Things as They are'. We can only make sense of morality if we recognise, first, the subjective nature of our own moral feelings and, secondly, that these feelings are striving to express objective moral values.

Psychology

Earlier in this chapter we saw A J Ayer's assertion, in *Language, Truth and Logic*, that ethical statements have no factual meaning. In holding this view, he was not denying that ethical sentiments exist or that they might be of some interest: he was saying that they lie outside the scope of philosophical enquiry, in the rather narrow sense understood by logical positivists. He went on to conclude that 'ethics, as a branch of knowledge, is nothing more than a department of psychology and sociology.'

Despite its disparaging tone ('nothing more than'), Ayer's point that ethics should be seen as a branch of psychology and sociology is a good one. The data of ethics are our moral sentiments, which, as part of the workings of the human mind, come under the scope of psychology. The moral sense is an important part of the human personality, an important influence on human behaviour, and central to the way we assess our own behaviour and that of other people. It should have a prominent place in the study of the human personality and human behaviour. Psychology and sociology could contribute a great deal to an understanding of the moral sense, and it is both surprising and regrettable that the moral dimension of the human personality has received so little attention in the mainstream of psychology.[2] The quotation at the beginning of this chapter should be part of the thinking of every psychologist and sociologist, but Frans de Waal comes from neither of these disciplines — he is a biologist who has specialised in the study of primate behaviour.

---

[2]   I use the term 'mainstream' to distinguish it from evolutionary psychology
      (see page 4). The latter discipline, which has its own literature, distinct
      from mainstream psychology, does recognise the moral dimension of the
      human personality, though it tends to have a rather limited view of it, more
      concerned to buttress a theory than to look at the facts with an open mind
      (see page 35).

To illustrate this point let us turn to the authoritative and otherwise excellent 1000-page second edition of *The Oxford Companion to the Mind* (Gregory, 2004), and look up conscience, ethics, guilt, morality, temptation and values. There are no entries under any of these headings. The first edition (1986) of this work contains an entry for 'Brain manipulation, ethics of'. Psychologists, it seems, are interested in the ethics of psychology, but not in the psychology of ethics. Ethical considerations mean something to them when they are thinking about their own professional conduct (Koocher and Keith-Spiegel, 1998, gives, in its 500 pages, numerous examples of situations that require ethical judgement), but it is curious that they are not meaningful to them when they are describing the human mind in general. Ethics has a place in their own practical, workaday lives, but, as theorists, they construct a model of the human personality in which ethical considerations have no part.

The picture in the social sciences is similar. *The Social Science Encyclopedia* (Kuper and Kuper, 1996), with 900 pages, contains no entries for conscience, ethics, guilt, morality or temptation. There is an entry for 'Ethics in social research', showing that social scientists are interested in the ethics of social science though not in the role of ethics in social behaviour. The 1989 edition has an entry on 'Moral Development', summarising the pioneering work of Piaget (1932) and Kohlberg (1981; Colby and others, 1983) in this field. It seems that the child's moral sense is thought to be so much more interesting than that of the adult; this is like studying how a child learns to play the flute, yet having no interest in the musicianship of the mature flautist.

This is psychology for psychologists. How about psychologists who communicated to the wider public? Few people have achieved more in this field than the American psychologist, Carl Rogers, who, more than anyone else, was responsible for the spread of the principles of counselling and psychotherapy to all the caring professions. His books, of which the most important is *Client-centred Therapy* (1951), display a positive and optimistic view of human nature (unlike Freud) and emphasise the motivation present in people to develop their full potential — but they have little to say about the moral sense or its importance as a motivating force giving sense and purpose to our lives. Indeed, his emphasis on the non-directive nature of his therapeutic approach joined with other influences to produce the concept of value-free therapy.

Another American writer, Thomas Harris, author of the best-selling *I'm OK — You're OK* (1967), on the other hand, is critical of psychologists and psychiatrists for their refusal to accept the existence of and need for a system of moral values. The idea of value-free therapy is now widely discredited, as therapists have come to see that the ethical convictions of the therapist and the client have much to contribute to the therapeutic process and should not be ignored (e.g. Kitwood, 1990; Tjeltveit, 1999). Therapy cannot be truly 'client-centred' unless it recognises the importance of the client's moral sentiments.

In contrast to the dearth of entries in *The Oxford Companion to the Mind*, *The Oxford Companion to Philosophy* (Honderich, 2005) has entries for conscience and guilt as well as numerous entries for ethics and numerous entries for moral philosophy (and even one for moral psychology). Most writers on morality have been philosophers, theologians and, in recent years, biologists with a particular interest in evolution. A recent edited volume, *Evolution and Ethics* (Clayton and Schloss, 2004) has 18 contributors from various disciplines, but not one of them is a psychologist. The result is a valuable presentation of current thinking on the subject, but it lacks a grounding in basic data about the nature and diversity of moral thinking. Indeed, one of the contributors (Haarsma, 2004) remarks that sociobiology and evolutionary psychology have theories well in advance of empirical data.

In fact, quite a lot of work on moral thinking has been done by psychologists, although it has been generally ignored by the mainstream. In *The Psychology of Moral Behaviour*, published in 1971, Derek Wright presents an introduction to the psychological study of moral behaviour and moral thinking, based on a discussion of empirical data obtained under controlled conditions. The purpose of his book is to understand how and why people differ in their moral behaviour. Most of the book is devoted to discussion of five variables (resistance to temptation, guilt, altruism, moral insight or reasoning, and moral ideology or beliefs) including the evidence for correlation with such variables as intelligence, sex and age. The author refers to an extensive literature on the subject, but he also notes that it is a subject that has been neglected by psychologists. This remains true (in spite of more recent publications such as Kitwood, 1990, Malan, 1995, and May and others, 1996), in that textbooks and other mainstream books on psychology have little or nothing to say about moral thinking; there may be a passing reference to the work of Piaget and Kohlberg, but little more.

Perhaps psychologists and sociologists were influenced by spirit of the age — or perhaps they helped to fashion the spirit of the age. The twentieth century was the age of subjectivist ethics, the permissive society, the compassionate society and the wish to understand rather to condemn; an age when, for sociologists, psychologists and the circles they moved in, it was out of fashion to talk of religion or the moral values traditionally associated with religion. Perhaps they felt that in an unbelieving age ethics was unimportant and, if God is left out of the picture, there are no agreed grounds for studying moral issues. Whatever the reason, it may be hoped that psychologists and sociologists will devote more attention to the study of the moral sense in the future.

Economics

Since humans are moral beings, moral considerations have a part to play in the economic decisions that we make: in how we spend our money, in our choice of employment, and in any unpaid or underpaid work we might do. Our public services and other organisations receive a great deal of help from volunteers, and the charitable sector makes a huge contribution to national life. The cooperative movement dates back to the nineteenth century, and in recent years the idea of social enterprise (businesses that trade for a social purpose; they may be charities, cooperatives or plcs, and include such diverse enterprises as *The Big Issue* and the Eden Project) has been gaining ground. Moral thinking is an important motivation behind all of these.

For much of the twentieth century, however, economics generally ignored the role of moral considerations in human economic behaviour — a remarkable omission. 'Can the people whom economics studies really ... stick exclusively to the rudimentary hard-headedness attributed to them by modern economics?' asks Nobel Prize winner Amartya Sen (1987). He goes on to draw attention to 'the contrast between the self-consciously "non-ethical" character of modern economics and the historical evolution of modern economics largely as an offshoot of ethics. Not only was the so-called "father of modern economics", Adam Smith, a Professor of Moral Philosophy at the University of Glasgow ... but the subject of economics was for a long time seen as something like a branch of ethics.'

At the political level, however, economic policies often claimed a moral basis. As with psychology and sociology, we can note a contrast between what was expected of practitioners (in this case, those responsible for formulating economic policies for the rest of us to live by) and what was expected of ordinary people. The former were expected to be motivated by moral considerations (a 'social conscience', for example) whereas the latter were expected to follow simple self-interest.

This denial of moral behaviour in economics may well be associated with the similar denial of the importance of moral considerations in philosophy and psychology. Sen (1987) points out that the 'peculiarly narrow view of "meaning" championed by the logical positivists — enough to cause disorder in philosophy itself — caused total chaos in welfare economics when it was supplemented by some additional home-grown confusions liberally supplied by economists themselves.' And not only in welfare economics: the denial of the moral dimension has interfered with the effective operation of the free-market economy as well (page 45).

2-2. Perspectives on the Moral Sense

I believe one should trust problems over solutions, intuition over arguments, and pluralistic discord over systematic harmony.

Thomas Nagel, *Mortal Questions*

It is outside the scope of this book to provide a comprehensive summary of moral philosophy: there are many textbooks and popular introductions to ethics that fulfill that purpose.[3] The aim of this section is to look at some of the ways in which it is possible to attempt an overview of the whole field of moral thinking, before we go on to consider specific issues in Chapter 3.

Upbringing

Freud considered that the moral sense is inculcated during one's upbringing, by parents and others, and psychology textbooks treat moral thinking, insofar as they consider it at all, as an aspect of childhood development.

It is true, of course, that we are taught moral values in childhood, but when we grow up we make our own decisions. Many people rebel, on moral grounds, against some aspects of their upbringing (it is quite common, for example, for young people to have a sense of moral indignation at inequalities in society, inequalities that are more readily accepted by their parents). This rebellion can start at quite an early age ('It's not fair: mummy and daddy are nicer to my brother than they are to me': note the appeal to the moral concept of fairness (see page 53). The child is not content with a subjective 'I am

[3] I particularly recommend *Ethics* (1994), edited by Peter Singer in the Oxford Readers series, which brings together important texts from a wide range of original sources, accompanied by Singer's easy-to-understand commentary. Mary Warnock (1998) and Simon Blackburn (2001) provide good introductions to moral philosophy. Mary Midgley (1991) discusses at greater length the difficulties associated with attempts to detract from the importance of moral judgement.

unhappy', or 'I don't like mummy and daddy' but wishes to invoke a wider moral principle). We decide to reject some of the values we received from our parents, teachers and other people, but we keep some of them and make them our own. A basic moral sense – a sense of right and wrong – is something we all keep, and we develop it during the course of our lives.

In *The Oxford Companion to the Mind* (Gregory, 2004), the section on 'ego and superego' contains the statement, 'The superego, manifest in conscience, shame and guilt, is the agency by which the influence of parents and others is prolonged.' If conscience were no more than that, the pleasure-seeking, mature adult would have no difficulty in rationalising it away and we would see a decline in moral thinking and moral behaviour as people grew to adulthood. This, however, is not normally the case. Most people use the moral teaching of their early years as a foundation on which to build their own set of values. An adult's moral values may be very similar to those taught in childhood, or they may be very different. As Noam Chomsky (1988) has written, 'it certainly seems reasonable to speculate that the moral and ethical system acquired by the child owes much to some innate human faculty.'

Feelings and Reason

Michael Gazzaniga is a neuroscientist with a particular interest in the contribution that brain science can make to ethics. And yet he found, in writing *The Ethical Brain* (2005), that he has a sense of ethics that is independent of rational science — a modern illustration of David Hume's (1739/40) 'Morality, therefore, is more properly felt than judg'd of'. The moral sense is akin to the feelings and emotions — though, as we have seen in Section 2-1, it differs from other feelings and emotions in that it carries with it a sense that it does not exist solely within ourselves but is in some way connected with something outside.

Immanuel Kant, while agreeing with Hume that the will to act in accordance with the moral law was essential to moral behaviour, put greater emphasis on the role of reasoning in our moral judgements. His view was that good deeds motivated by naturally kindly, loving and altruistic feelings are of no moral worth: 'an act has moral worth only in so far as it is done out of a sense of duty — that is, out of respect for the pure moral law in itself' (Singer, 1994). This argument carries some weight. To refrain from stealing money when I have neither the desire nor the opportunity, for example, is hardly a triumph of moral muscle; whereas if I refrain from stealing when I have both the desire and the opportunity (I won't be caught, no one will know, and the firm, with its multi-million pound turnover, won't be hurt by the loss of £100), the moral sense is proving its power to influence my decisions and my behaviour. It is a convenience in everyday speech to describe an act of kindness, performed by a human or some other animal, as 'good', whatever the motive, but it is only when the act is performed contrary to the natural impulses that the uniquely human attribute, the moral sense, is apparent.

This rather pedantic viewpoint helps to clarify the nature of the moral sense, but it should not be used to belittle the good deed done out of sheer benevolence, nor to devalue the sentiments of kindliness. A generous deed may reflect a generous sentiment, or it may demonstrate an ability to overcome a natural meanness. It can be argued, contrary to Kant, that what matters is the good deed; motives can be complex and mercurial, and are often too insubstantial to form the basis of a moral judgement.

If we agree that we want to lead moral lives, it would seem no more than sensible that we should encourage generosity in ourselves and discourage meanness (for example), since this will make it easier, and more likely, that we will act generously. Thus, we may hope to build up our character so that we will automatically act in a moral way, without the need for deliberation. According to Kant's view, such actions will be of no moral worth, but it would seem rather perverse to encourage the meaner side of our nature in order to strengthen our moral resolve, so that our generosity should have greater worth. However much we might admire the person who strives successfully to overcome a powerful inner meanness, we would probably feel that a natural generosity was morally preferable.

In some situations the moral sense may be all that is required to produce appropriate moral action: in others a process of reasoning may be necessary. If I am tempted to steal some money, the moral sense may be enough to prevent me from doing so: no reasoning is required. Other situations may call for detailed analysis of the circumstances, followed by careful consideration of the moral issues involved and the likely consequences of various possible courses of action. There need be no conflict between feeling-based and reason-based theories of ethics. The wish to do what is right is a feeling, and so is the sense that X is the right course of action. The role of reason is to check that X really is right (check against any wider moral law that I might adhere to, against the views of the community of which I am a part, and against my own judgement and any contrary moral feelings that I might have). Without the innate moral sense, there is no ethics. Without reason, a supposedly moral response to a situation may turn out to be disastrously wrong. We need 'a judicious admixture of intuitive and critical thinking' (Hare, 1989).

David Hume (1739/40) famously wrote that you cannot derive an 'ought' from an 'is'. We can describe a situation as it is (there is an abandoned toddler in the road, for example), but if we then go on to say that something ought to be done about it we are doing more than embellishing our description: we are making an assumption about moral values. We might think that some statements of value are so obvious that they go without saying ('happiness is better than unhappiness', for example, or 'kindness is better than cruelty'), but such basic statements of value form an essential part of the argument and if we omit them and try to infer the 'ought' directly from the 'is' we are guilty of what G E Moore (1903) called the 'naturalistic fallacy'.

Principles versus Consequences

Some philosophers judge the morality of an act by its consequences, others judge according to some moral principle. The principle of consequentialism is derived from Jeremy Bentham's philosophy of utilitarianism: 'The greatest happiness of the greatest number is the foundation of morals and legislation'. Happiness is not the only good that is worth aiming for, however, and so the term 'consequentialism' is used for moral thinking that includes consideration of all possible consequences of an action. Consequentialism depends on an understanding of what consequences are desirable and what is undesirable, and therefore it cannot exist without the acknowledgement of some sort of moral principle.

Moral principle is more closely related to the ingrained moral sense. It may be based on authority, such as religious teaching or the values of the society we live in, or on some philosophical principle. Alternatively, it may simply be based on unexamined and unquestioned inner moral convictions.

Very often, in daily life, moral principle and consequentialist thinking lead to the same conclusions. Moral principle says that we should tell the truth; the consequence of habitual lying and deceit is a breakdown of trust and effective communication. Moral principle says we should not commit murder; the consequences of murder include the loss of life of the victim, the grief of those who are bereaved, and, if murder is widespread in a community, fearfulness and the breakdown of trust. Moral principle says we should not steal; the consequences of theft include the loss to the victim and, again, anxiety and the breakdown of trust.

Sometimes, however, consequentialist thinking comes into conflict with moral principle. It is not uncommon for circumstances to arise in which telling the truth can have unfortunate consequences — in causing needless hurt, for example — though few of us experience the classic philosophers' example of being asked by a would-be murderer to tell him where he can find his intended victim.

A stark and well-documented example of conflict between moral principle and consequentialist moral thinking is given by the decision by the climber Simon Yates to cut the rope linking him to his friend Joe Simpson (Simpson, 1988; Yates, 1997). The two men had accomplished the first ascent of the west face of the 6356 m Siula Grande in the Peruvian Andes and had started to descend when Simpson fell and broke his leg. Yates tried to get him to safety by lowering him again and again on 300 feet of rope, but eventually, with Simpson dangling helplessly at the end of the rope and Yates himself in danger of being dragged down with him, he cut the rope. He returned to camp, convinced that his friend was dead, but, amazingly, Simpson survived the fall and reached camp after an epic three-day crawl — one of the great survival stories of mountaineering.

Looking at Yates' momentous decision from a consequentialist perspective, (1) the expected consequences of not cutting the rope were that both men would have died, (2) the expected consequences of cutting the rope were that Yates would have lived and Simpson would have died, and (3) the actual consequences of cutting the rope were that both men lived. Taking the consequentialist line, there is therefore no doubt that Yates was right to cut the rope. And yet, the cutting of the rope, a deliberate action which, as he thought, would send his friend to certain death while saving his own life, offends against moral principle; even the feeling that he did right did not keep away the waves of fear, remorse and guilt as he walked away from the mountain. The knowledge that he did, in fact, save his friend's life as well as his own does not take away from the moral horror of that decisive act. Most climbers, including Simpson himself, have said that Yates was right to cut the rope, and that they would have done the same (judging from a consequentialist standpoint), though some have been critical (feeling, presumably, that the moral principle is so strong that to send someone to his death cannot be justified by a consequentialist argument).

A mature ethic should include both moral principle and a recognition of the value of consequentialist thinking. Principle sometimes needs to be tempered by consideration of consequences. A moral system based on consideration of consequences, on the other hand, is not viable without moral principles to state that a particular outcome is 'good' or 'bad' and to enable choices to be made between one 'good' outcome and another.

A difficulty with consequentialism is that the full consequences may not be known at the time that the decision is made. A slight distortion of the truth in order to improve a story may seem to be justified by its consequences (if it provides greater entertainment for the audience, for example), but there may be other, longer-term consequences in a breakdown of trust if it cannot be taken for granted that a person is speaking the truth. Aesop's 'Boy who cried Wolf' was pleased with the intended consequences of his little deceit, when people came running to save him from a wolf, only to find that there was no wolf; he did not foresee the longer-term consequence — that when he really was in danger from a wolf people assumed he was lying and therefore did not come to help him.

One of the strengths of consequentialism is that there is the opportunity for debate between different viewpoints. It therefore has an important role in social and political thinking: indeed, Jeremy Bentham and John Stuart Mill, the founders of utilitarianism, were social theorists and economists. Decisions about war or about government spending, for example, are assessed by considering their likely outcome — in the context of a consensus that it is the purpose of government to promote peace and prosperity.

The Role of Altruism

Humans are social beings, and altruism is a sound basis for social living. Altruism underlies many of the aspects of moral thinking that we shall look at in Chapter 3. However, it is not synonymous with the moral sense.

First, there is more to altruism than just moral behaviour. Altruism can come from the discipline of a moral sense overruling more self-centred inclinations, but it can also arise from a naturally caring nature or impulse, regardless of moral considerations. Other species, as well as humans, show the latter, though only humans display the former.

Secondly, many deeds of cruelty have been perpetrated in obedience to a (misguided?) moral sense: revenge, for example, and punishment that most readers of this book would regard as grossly excessive. The moral sense can thus include sentiments that are far from altruistic.

Finally, there is another sense in which there is more to moral behaviour than just altruism. Although humans are social creatures

we are also individuals, each with our own unique, solitary journey
through life. The moral sense has an important part to play in this
journey (see the section on personal integrity, page 78).

The Role of Religion

The will of God

To the believer, all things come from God, but that is not to say that
the moral sense is infallible, providing us with a direct line to God's
law. Believers may hope that our moral sense leads us to seek the
will of God, but not everything that the moral sense tells us is necessarily the will of God. People often disagree on matters of moral
principle sufficiently seriously for it not to be possible that both
views are from God. Moreover, Christians will note that Jesus himself said to his friends and followers that 'an hour is coming when
those who kill you will think that by doing so they are offering wor-
ship to God' (John 16:2). Sincere moral convictions can be cata-
strophically wrong, even when people are convinced that their
moral beliefs are from God. Then again, Christians will also note
that some of our deep moral convictions are contrary to the teach-
ings of the New Testament (see pages 71–73).

Religion and morality

Is the moral sense inextricably bound up with religious faith, or are
they separate? For much of the Christian era, there was little doubt
in the minds of Christians that the two were closely associated: virtue and godliness were considered to be much the same thing, as
were evil and ungodliness. During the nineteenth century, however, unbelief came to be recognised as a reasonable way of looking
at the world. It had become respectable, and there were people who
took exception to the traditional view, advanced by believers, that
'only God could define good and evil, and that only the fear of God
could make men do good and shun evil. No, replied Huxley and
John Stuart Mill and George Eliot and Bagehot; *we* are plainly all
people of the highest rectitude; and therefore the moral sense must
be inborn in every man' (Bronowski, 1949). As the Christian theologian Alec Vidler (1965) put it, 'Honest Christians could hardly deny
the shining moral integrity of the noble army of Victorian
agnostics.'

Other people, in contrast, have emphasised that freedom from
belief in God led to freedom from external moral pressures. 'Man is
condemned to be free', wrote Sartre (1946), and Dostoevsky is
widely quoted, 'If God did not exist, everything would be permit-

ted'. A J Ayer (1936) also considered that moral behaviour was closely associated with religious belief: 'one of the chief causes of moral behaviour is fear, both conscious and unconscious, of a god's displeasure, and fear of the enmity of society.'

The existence of highly moral non-believers and of morally bad deeds performed by people who claim to have a religious faith supports the view that religious faith and moral sense are different entities (two different dimensions, perhaps), and I consider that it is valid to examine the one without the other, as in this book. We should recognise, however, that for many people the two are inseparable: 'What is the right thing for me to do?' and 'What is God's will for me?' are different ways of expressing the same sentiment.

Religion and a secular moral code

For believers, their moral principles are closely bound up with their religious faith, but a great deal of moral thinking today is divorced from religious belief and it is widely acknowledged, by believers and non-believers alike, that we need to establish some kind of moral consensus that is not founded on religion.

Some broadcasts by Margaret Knight (a non-believer) in 1955 on moral education separated from religion attracted a great deal of attention, as did a book by Richard Holloway (a bishop), published in 1999, which aimed 'to unite those who believe with those who do not in the discovery of a workable ethic of our time.' Other writers with a similar message include the educationalist Paul Hirst (1974), who argued for 'a secularised approach to the moral life ... characterised by rational autonomy' and the philosopher Roger Scruton (1996) who wrote of the urgency 'to address moral questions in terms which make no theological assumptions'. This is the likely way forward for our society. People with religious faith will continue to be guided by their faith in their own personal lives, but religious teaching will not be accepted by non-believers as a basis for legislation and socially acceptable behaviour. Teaching and ideas expressed by religious leaders may well be regarded as useful contributions to debate, but they will carry no privileged authority on account of their religious provenance.

The removal of religious beliefs from the picture could help us to find enough common ground to hold constructive debates on moral issues, but it will not put an end to disagreements. Many issues will remain controversial even when religious considerations have been left out of account, but there are likely to be non-believers on both sides of each debate — and in many issues there will be believers on both sides as well. Points of view will be based on individual moral sentiments or convictions, many of which are shared by believers and non-believers. We shall consider the basis for such a moral consensus in Chapter 4.

Human Rights

The concept of human rights has a long history, but it was only during the second half of the twentieth century that the idea arose that human rights could form the basis of a moral system. This was a time when people were uncomfortable with traditional expressions of morality (as discussed in Section 2-1), so perhaps the human-rights concept filled a gap: it enabled people to give expression to their natural moral instincts in a way that was socially acceptable.

It may have been attractive in other ways as well. First, by emphasising our rights rather than our duties it appealed to the 'me first' side of human nature. Secondly, rights were mostly political in nature, as exemplified by the United Nations' Universal Declaration of Human Rights. Insofar as anybody was responsible for satisfying a person's human rights this responsibility rested with governments. It is a very comfortable form of morality, if it makes no demands of me: all I have to do is to express my moral indignation at the deficiencies of governments all round the world.

Attractive and socially acceptable it may be, but the idea of a rights-based moral system does not stand up to scrutiny (e.g. Warnock, 1998; Taylor, 2004). First, human rights are arbitrary — anybody can claim a right, and there are no criteria for deciding between two that are in conflict (the right of a woman to have an abortion, for example, against the right of a foetus to live; or the individual's right to privacy against the public's right to know). In order to resolve these conflicts, it is necessary to refer to the principles and methods of moral philosophy. Secondly, a right is worthless without a corresponding obligation. As Mary Warnock points out, 'Whenever a right is claimed one is entitled … to raise the question, "Who or what conferred it?"' As a list of ideals, the United Nations' Universal Declaration of Human Rights is very commendable, but the concept of 'rights' suggests more than an ideal. It suggests that they are attainable, that there is somebody there to provide whatever it is that people are entitled to. Some such rights, such as the right to education or the right to work for just and favourable remuneration (or compensating social protection) only make sense in countries where the government has the resources to provide its people with these 'rights'. A right becomes more than an ideal when it is enshrined in law: the right to ownership of property, for example, or the right to use the public highway. Such rights have their basis, and their definition, in legislation, not in moral philosophy.

To me, morality is about what I should do — very often what I should do for other people. The human-rights concept turns this upside down and places the emphasis on what other people should do for me. The former places moral responsibility where it belongs, on me; the latter on some unidentified other. In this sense, therefore, the concept of human rights has no place in moral philosophy.

A list of human rights like the United Nations' Universal Declaration of Human Rights has a moral basis, in that we feel it is morally right to care about the material well-being of other people, wherever they are. The idea of human rights is thus derived from our moral sense, and we turn this relationship upside down if we try to use the rights concept as the foundation for a moral system. Whatever authority the human-rights concept has, it derives from the moral sense. Being derivative rather than authoritative, it cannot form the basis of a moral system. To find the basis of such a system, we must return to the source — to our own innate moral sense.

Evolution

Our animal ancestry

Humans, like all living organisms, have an ancestry that stretches back to the earliest life forms nearly 4 billion years ago. Each species contains many of the features of its parent species, as well as some significant differences. The evidence for inheritance of physical characteristics is obtained from fossils, combined with comparative studies of the anatomy of living species. Important supporting evidence is now obtained from studies of DNA. This idea of evolution based on inheritance was widely discussed in the years before the publication in 1859 of Charles Darwin's *The Origin of Species*.

The same principle can be applied to behaviour. Behaviour itself is not preserved in fossils, though physical features of fossils and the environment in which ancient animals lived can tell us a great deal about lifestyle and some aspects of behaviour. Most of the evidence for inheritance of behavioural traits therefore comes from the study of living species, and the more we study animal behaviour the more we see how similar human behaviour is to that of other species. To understand the human inheritance, we need to look at other animals, in particular chimpanzees and other apes. When certain behaviour patterns are commonly seen in other animals as well as in humans, it may be reasonable to suggest that, like physical features, the propensity for this behaviour is inherited from our pre-human primate ancestors.

The moral sense motivates human behaviour and makes judgements about it. It interacts with our inherited patterns of behaviour and thinking, as we shall see in Chapter 3.

Natural selection

The principle of natural selection is also known as 'survival of the fittest'.[4] This prompts the question, 'Fittest for what?', to which the reply is 'Fittest for survival, of course.' So, this principle states that those individuals best fitted to survive are the ones that survive. It was Charles Darwin's genius that he took this simple statement of the obvious and, with a well-presented argument and a mass of illustrative evidence, set out to show, in *The Origin of Species*, how it could make sense of the enormous diversity of living organisms and their evolution from the earliest life forms right up to the present day: given the natural genetic variability within any population, individuals with features that favour survival in the prevailing environment are more likely to survive to adulthood and breed successfully; their offspring will inherit the favoured feature; repeated over many generations, this results in the favoured feature being present in the entire population. Any mutations that give rise to features that are seriously injurious to survival are not perpetuated (Darwin actually put it more strongly: 'any variation in the least degree injurious would be rigidly destroyed'). Variations that are neither useful nor injurious are not affected by natural selection. Darwin gave examples to show that natural selection operated both on physical features and on instinctive behaviour.

Darwin knew nothing of the modern science of genetics, of course. 'The only section of *The Origin of Species* which does not make good reading today is Chapter Five, "Laws of variation"' (Jones, 2000). His purpose in *The Origin of Species* was to demonstrate the significance of natural selection, but he was at pains to emphasise that he did not regard it as the exclusive means of modification. In the last edition (1872) he concluded that he had underrated the frequency and value of 'variations which seem to us in our ignorance to arise spontaneously'. The geneticist Gabriel Dover takes up this latter point in an imagined correspondence between himself and Darwin, explaining how current thinking about genetics can be related to Darwin's own ideas (Dover, 2000a):

---

[4]   The phrase 'survival of the fittest' was originated by Herbert Spencer, and subsequently used by Darwin in later editions of *The Origin of Species*.

But there is more to the origins and spread of successful biological novelties than natural selection … [N]ew forms can arise through a combination of internal pressures generated by the unruly genes (molecular drive) and external pressures generated by an unruly environment (natural selection). Darwin focused on the latter mechanism, as the former was not known to him.

There is a difference between the role of the 'unruly genes' and that of the environment, in that it is changes in the genes that actually produce the inheritable novelties; what natural selection does is to weed out, quickly or slowly, those novelties which lack the fitness to survive and breed successfully in a competitive environment.

There is a great deal more to learn (see, for example, Dover, 2000a,b and extracts in Ridley, 1997). Different genes cooperate to produce proteins (thousands of proteins in each cell), and proteins themselves can have multiple roles in the body. Human DNA contains some three billion chemical base pairs, and there are thought to be about 25,000 genes in the human genome. If these numbers are compared with the 100 billion nerve cells (neurons) in the human brain and the 100 trillion synapses that link them (Rose, 2005) it is clear that the relationships between genetic material and the substances that make up the body must be very complex. The relationships between genes and physical features are only sketchily known, and those between genes, the physical brain and mental processes scarcely understood at all, apart from those known to be associated with severe hereditary defects (Ehrlich, 2000).

The presence of a feature in some individuals in a population is not proof that it has survival value. Other scenarios include: (1) a feature that is neither helpful nor injurious to survival is not affected by natural selection; (2) an attribute that is itself neutral, or even injurious, may be genetically associated with another attribute that is beneficial (the classic example is sickle-cell anaemia in humans, a life-threatening condition which is genetically associated with protection against malaria and is therefore favoured, to some extent, by natural selection in areas where malaria is prevalent; Allison, 1954a,b); (3) a feature that is mildly injurious may be the result of a common mutation, so that, although natural selection works (slowly) against it, it is always present in a significant proportion of the individuals in a population; and (4) a feature that is injurious may be so favoured by a process that is stronger or faster than natural selection that it prospers in spite of natural selection (like the peacock's tail, favoured by sexual selection; Darwin, 1872, 1874; Cronin, 1991; Ridley, 1993).

One type of behaviour that is particularly relevant to the subject of this book is caring and nurturing the young. In animal species in which the newborn young are unable to take care of themselves it is vital for survival that they should be fed, nurtured and protected until they can fend for themselves. As Richard Dawkins (1976) points out, 'The commonest and most conspicuous acts of animal altruism are done by parents, especially mothers, towards their children.'

This is readily accounted for by natural selection: the offspring of parents that did not have this behaviour would not survive to breed, so the genetic propensity to let one's offspring die would not survive. However, it is not uncommon for animals to nurture young animals that are not their own offspring: behaviour that is contrary to the principle of natural selection. It is not the survival of their own chicks and their own genes that leads meadow pipits to feed and nurture the young cuckoo in the nest — the bird that has, in effect, murdered their own offspring — but this is not the point. The point is that feeding young chicks is what meadow pipits do: give them a hungry chick in the nest and they'll feed it. In another example, Robert Sapolsky (2001) tells of a baboon who risked his life to save two young baboons from a lion, even though they were not his own offspring. Jane Goodall (1990) gives examples of chimpanzees taking similar risks for unrelated chimpanzees and suggests that such behaviour derives from the more usual behaviour of caring for kin: 'From these basically selfish roots [i.e. caring for one's own young and kin] sprang the most rarefied form of altruism — helping another even when you stand to gain nothing for yourself or your kin.'

Thus caring, most especially for the young, vulnerable and needy, is what many animals do (and humans more than others), simply because it is in their nature. We can see an evolutionary process at work, in the sense that such caring seems to have developed gradually, starting with the earliest instances of parental care, millions of years ago, and culminating in the kind of practical caring concern that leads present-day humans to help with, and contribute to, famine relief overseas and wildlife hospitals at home. It is an evolutionary process, but it is not natural selection. Indeed, it is contrary to the principle of natural selection, for if natural selection were the dominant influence, 'a gene for kin-unrelated altruism ... would be automatically selected against' (in the words of Colin McGinn, 1979; but see the discussion on reciprocal altruism on page 44). Compassion that is concentrated particularly on the weak, sick and vulnerable operates in direct opposition to the Malthus-Darwin principle that in a competitive environment, where there is not enough food to go round, the strongest and fittest individuals are the ones that survive. Caring that extends to the weak and vulnerable and to those who are not our kin — or even our own species — is not favoured by natural selection (Sapolsky remarks of his brave baboon (above) that he showed 'how little he understood modern evolutionary thinking'), but it appears to be favoured by some other evolutionary process, and is not so injurious to survival that it has been selected against (see Goodall, 1990; Wilson, 1993; Midgley, 1995; de Waal, 2001).

The tyranny of evolutionary correctness

I drew attention on page 32 to a difference between what Darwin wrote about natural selection ('any variation in the least degree injurious would be rigidly destroyed') and my own preference ('Any mutations that give rise to features that are seriously injurious to survival are not perpetuated'). This seemingly small difference in wording is, in fact, of immense significance. If we follow Darwin here, we are led to the view that natural selection determines, in every detail, what features will prosper. It follows that if we see that a particular feature (physical or behavioural) has prospered, it can only be because it has helped survival. There is no escaping the logic, once you accept the premise. It is a 'universal acid', to quote Daniel Dennett's (1995) phrase. This view of natural selection is to be found in many writings on sociobiology and evolutionary psychology, and it has become widely promoted as a doctrine to which all right-thinking people must assent — a doctrine that I shall call evolutionary correctness. As Mary Midgley (1995) puts it, 'Serious scientific articles, as well as TV programmes about animals, now all have an obligatory section proving that the behaviour discussed — however obviously futile it may be — must have been selectively advantageous to the creature's ancestors, since sociobiological theory insists that it must be so.'

Evolutionary correctness has its own imperative (if it aids biological fitness, it will be perpetuated; if not, not), and it allows room for no imperative and no values but its own. That is why it has a particular problem with morality. Morality has its own values and purposes, which are fundamentally different from those of natural selection. Morality is about idealism, personal autonomy and personal fulfilment, whereas natural selection is about survival and breeding. Evolutionary correctness cannot accept morality, therefore, and tries to come to terms with it by redefining it. If morality only consists of such altruistic behaviour as aids evolutionary fitness, then it can be accepted as a product of natural selection.

There is no need for us to accept the tyranny of evolutionary correctness, however (see, for example, the 15 contributions to Rose and Rose, 2000). Both theory and observation support the view set out on the preceding pages, recognising the role of natural selection in weeding out the worst, but also allowing other processes to play their part in shaping evolution. In every edition of *The Origin of Species* Darwin himself clearly stated his belief that natural selection was not the only process involved in evolution, and in the 1872 (and last) edition he expressed his displeasure at the way that his views had been misrepresented by those who stated that he attributed the modification of species exclusively to natural selection. When we consider the strength of Darwin's advocacy of natural selection we might not be surprised that he should have been misunderstood in this way, but he himself saw it as a serious misrepresentation of his views. Natural selection is an extremely important process, but there are other things going on as well. This applies most of all to humans and their behaviour. 'For even though we and our capacities may have evolved in Darwinian ways, once evolved we and our capacities take off in quite un-Darwinian ways' (Anthony O'Hear, 1997).

How does the moral sense relate to this? Caring and nurturing behaviour is well established in animals that have no moral sense, and it therefore seems reasonable to suppose that it was well developed in our ancestors before our species acquired a moral sense. At some point our ancestors began to experience moral sentiments, recognise temptation and make moral judgements, and this new capacity engaged with the human propensity for caring, as well as other aspects of the human personality, as described in Chapter 3. It was Darwin's opinion (1874) that an animal with the social instincts and intellect of human beings would inevitably acquire a moral sense. His use of the word 'inevitably' suggests the logic of evolutionary correctness, and we shall examine this further in Chapter 4.

Conclusions

All of the approaches considered in this section help us to understand the moral mind. Each is helpful, but none of them is fully adequate to explain or account for everything that we know about the moral sense. In Chapter 3 we shall examine various manifestations of moral thinking, and we shall see to what extent they fit into the perspectives that have been outlined in this chapter. But first there are some general issues concerning choice to be considered.

2-3. Morality Means Choice

[T]he moral point of view is the one where we consider priorities, where we ask, 'what are the most serious, the central things in life?'

Mary Midgley, *Heart and Mind*

Temptation

The existence of a moral sense does not lead automatically to morally good behaviour. When there are choices to be made, the result is not a foregone conclusion. This means that, where morality and moral choices exist, temptation and wrongdoing are there as well. We have the potential for conflict between our natural emotions and impulses and our understanding of right and wrong. The idea of temptation seldom gets a mention in modern discussions of the human personality, but it is central to any concept of morality, a necessary and integral part of what it is to be a moral being. If there is no temptation, there is no morality, for if everybody automatically does what is right on every occasion there is no moral choice.

Today the concept of temptation may be particularly associated with traditional Christian teaching, but Aristotle also recognised the conflict between what we may want to do and the 'right principle' within us; weakness of will means that the 'right principle' sometimes loses the battle. In Book 7 of the *Nichomachean Ethics*, he suggests that it may be possible to distinguish between the temperate man, who does good deeds naturally and easily, and the continent man, who succeeds in doing good deeds against contrary inclinations.

Human beings have many natural wants and impulses, and these emotions can be unpredictable and uncontrollable. Some of them can be described as good; some are, by any standards, bad; and many of them are morally neutral. To those who ask whether human nature is fundamentally good or fundamentally bad, the answer is that we are both. Human nature is full of opposites. We are competitive and cooperative, aggressive and peaceable, conformist and autonomous, and selfish as well as altruistic (Talbot, 2005). We are all a mixture. The human mind is not a computer (Tallis, 2004). In all kinds of ways, from anxiety and depression to simple forgetfulness and lack of concentration, the mind takes us down roads that we would rather not travel and it fails to give us the emotions, the will power and the rationality that we would wish to have at our command. There is therefore no reason for surprise that we should find our minds leading us away from what we know to be morally right. In other words, temptation is a natural part of the human personality. Everybody experiences it, to a greater or lesser extent, and it is not always successfully resisted. We have moral ideals, and we know that we fail to live up to them. This knowledge is central to the human predicament, and leads us to explore the great religious themes of forgiveness, judgement and redemption.

We are all alike in experiencing temptation, but we are all different in the particular blend of natural impulses, emotions and restraints that make up our individual personalities. When we see faults in others we are recognising that they are human, like ourselves, though their faults may be different.

Good versus Good

Not every moral action results from a struggle against temptation, however. Not every moral decision involves a stark choice between good and evil. Much of moral thinking involves weighing up two or more courses of action, all of which we think are 'good'.

Two people ask us to do something for them. We would like to oblige them both and our moral sense tells us that we should, but time only permits us to agree to one of the requests. Which do we do? Questions of temptation, sin and evil do not arise here, but we do have to make a moral decision. The choice may be dictated by a moral principle (family first, for example) or by a morally based consideration of the consequences.

Can We Really Choose?

I have assumed so far that we have free will and are able to make moral choices. Without the ability to make choices we are mere automata, driven by forces over which we have no control, and the belief that we can make moral choices, or any other decisions, is an illusion. Without free will we are not responsible for our actions — or, indeed, our thoughts.

We believe that we have free will, that we are free to make our own decisions — but are we deluding ourselves? The philosophical and theological aspects of this question have been debated down the ages. The growth of scientific understanding since Newton has enabled new arguments to join the debate: that every event, including every mental process, is determined by forces that are, at least potentially, within the understanding of science. The arguments are many and varied, and they are complicated by the lack of agreement about the meaning of the terms used. To take one example, the kind of biological determinism that holds that behaviour is controlled with absolute certainty by our genes only exists, according to

Steven Pinker (2002), in the minds of its opponents; no sane biologist would actually hold this view.

More generally, scientific determinism is based on the idea that all mental processes are caused by physical processes in the brain. The brain is a physical object, just chemical substances and electrical impulses, so the argument runs, and physical objects don't have free will. The mind is simply a product of the brain, so the mind can't have free will either. Thus, we cannot be held responsible for our actions, morality has no meaning and the concept of punishment for misconduct is called into question. This argument seems to divide humanity into two classes: 'them', who have no free will, cannot help what they are doing and should not be held responsible, and 'us' who write books about them and can debate whether or not wrongdoing should be punished — implying that, unlike them, we do have free will and can be held responsible.

The trouble with these deterministic lines of argument, it seems to me, is that they take very complicated areas of science, of which our understanding is far from complete, distort them in order to make them sound really simple, and use these false premises to support conclusions that are contrary to common sense.

Interestingly, Thomas Henry Huxley, an early champion of Darwin's theory of evolution by natural selection, was himself a convinced determinist but was equally definite that the scientific argument had nothing useful to contribute to the debate:

> Finally, if the belief in the uncausedness of volition is essential to morality, the student of physical science has no more to say against that absurdity than the logical philosopher or theologian. Physical science, I repeat, did not invent determinism, and the deterministic doctrine would stand on just as firm a foundation as it does if there were no physical science.[5]

Since Huxley's time we have learnt a great deal about physical and biological science, and we have learnt about the uncertainties inherent in the natural world at the subatomic level. We know, too, that there is a great deal that we do not understand about the interactions between mind, brain and genetics. The belief that all our thoughts and actions are determined by processes within the grasp of physical science is not proved, is not supported by evidence and is a matter of personal faith (Taylor, 2004).

Most of us for most of the time are responsible for our decisions and our actions. That is not to say, however, that we are all equally

---

[5]   From *Science and Morals*, an essay written in 1886 and published in Huxley (1895).

culpable when we get things wrong. Every human being experiences temptation and sometimes succumbs. Every human being is different, and it need come as no surprise that some people have unusually powerful temptations and lack the inner resources to overcome them. At the simplest level, we all know that there are times when it is easy to be kind or truthful, say, and times when it is not so easy. We can distinguish between a realistic recognition that human thought and behaviour are subject to all kinds of influences — influences which can, at times, be overwhelmingly powerful and can, in many cases, be partially understood by science — and a mechanistic determinism that allows no room for free will under any circumstances.

I do not propose to go into this complicated subject any further, but would refer the reader to recent discussions by Young (1991), Warnock (1998), Blackburn (2001), Pinker (2002), Hinde (2002) and Gazzaniga (2005).

Choice and Selfishness

It is sometimes argued that everything we do is done out of self-interest, in one way or another. Actions described as unselfish can provide us with a sense of satisfaction just as great as — or perhaps even greater than — actions described as selfish. If we perform a kind or generous deed it is because we have our own reasons for wanting to do so — even if those reasons are no more than that it makes us feel good, by bolstering our self-image (or our image in the eyes of other people) as a kind or generous person. These deeds are performed out of self-interest, the argument goes, and there is no such thing as unselfishness.

There is some truth in this argument — but it is not particularly helpful. We know that there is a moral difference between kindness and cruelty, between generosity and meanness, and we know what we mean when we describe someone's behaviour as selfish or unselfish. To say that everything we do is 'selfish' is to distort the meaning of the word. The definition given in the *Concise Oxford Dictionary* is 'concerned *chiefly* with one's own personal profit or pleasure *at the expense of consideration for others*' (my italics). The second part of the definition is critical to the way the word is normally used. It is not a concern for my own interests that makes my conduct 'selfish': I only become selfish if I fail to consider other people. An arrangement between two people that benefits them both is not selfishness, in this sense.

We thus have two meanings of the word 'selfish'. According to one definition I am being selfish if I get any benefit out of whatever I am doing. According to the other, the dictionary definition, I am only being selfish if I fail to consider other people. The former is used if the speaker wants to denigrate any kindly, moral or altruistic action ('Your generosity wasn't really unselfish: you only did it because you wanted to.') — but a word that has been defined in a way that fails to recognise any difference between the pleasure I get out of being kind and the pleasure I get from being cruel is of little use in moral discourse.

Chapter 3

Manifestations of Morality

In this chapter we shall look at various manifestations of the moral sense and the way that it interacts with other aspects of the human personality. Each section covers a different kind of thinking, with a different role for moral thinking. Any attempt like this to classify or make generalisations about something as complex as the human personality is bound to be an oversimplification. There will be overlaps and exceptions. Nevertheless, I hope that the distinctions made in these three sections will be helpful in coming to an understanding of the moral mind.

3-1. The Morality of Instinct: Our Animal Ancestry

> [O]bligations of kinship, reciprocity, and sexual relationships form the core of all human ethical systems — and they also guide the behaviour of our close non-human relatives.
>
> Peter Singer, *Ethics*

Although humans are the only species capable of moral thinking, other animals show patterns of behaviour which, to outward appearances, are very similar to our 'moral' behaviour. We describe animal behaviour as 'good', if, according to our moral judgement, we would describe similar behaviour in humans as 'good'. Frans de Waal's book *Good Natured: The Origins of Right and Wrong In Humans and Other Animals*, published in 1996, discusses this common ground between humans and other species, and the subject is further explored by the contributors to Katz (2000). When similar patterns of behaviour are present in humans and other animals, particularly our near-relations the apes, it is reasonable to suppose that they were also present in our common ancestors and that we can regard such behaviour patterns as instincts inherited from our pre-human ancestors.

In this section we shall look at aspects of human behaviour which we regard as within the scope of morality but which are similar to behaviour seen in other species, and we shall observe how our moral sense engages with this behaviour. We shall also consider fairness and guilt, which are ways of thinking rather than ways of behaving but which may have their roots, I suggest, in the psychology of our pre-human ancestors.

Family First

Care of the young is essential for the survival of those species in which parents only produce a small number of progeny. Mammals and birds, in particular, need to feed and protect their offspring if they are to survive. This behaviour is obviously favoured by natural selection.

More widely, many species live, for at least part of their lives, in family groups of one kind or another, and individuals take care of kin more than they do of other individuals. In the chimpanzees of Gombe, for example, most risk taking is on behalf of family members and so is caring for the sick (Goodall, 1990). To quote Frans de Waal (1996): 'In species after species, we see signs of kin selection: altruism is disproportionately directed at relatives. Humans are no exception.' Jane Goodall tells of one of the Gombe chimps who would bring food for her old and infirm mother.

In humans, we take it for granted that people favour their own kin, that families stick together. In the ordinary way, we hardly regard this as a moral issue, except that we disapprove of people when they neglect family members. Morality becomes a more real issue when some other moral principle comes into conflict with our obligation towards family. If a family member has broken the law, for example, and our civic duty requires that we inform and cooperate with the police, there may be a moral conflict between civic duty and family loyalty.

Family first seems to be an example of inherited behaviour, which, because it is part of our normal pattern of living, came to be regarded as 'good' when humans acquired the ability to make moral judgements.

Caring for Other Young and Vulnerable Animals

Animals can show a caring disposition towards young that are not their own. We have already met Robert Sapolsky's baboon (page 34). Jane Goodall (1990) tells of an orphan chimpanzee who was adopted by an unrelated male. To take another example, when a female avocet at a nature reserve in Lincolnshire died after laying her clutch of four eggs in 2001, a second male helped the father to rear the young and fend off predatory gulls (*Birds*, Spring 2002).

This caring disposition extends to the young of other species. Adult animals can rear the young of other species, both in nature (as when meadow pipits rear the young cuckoo in the nest) and in captivity (as in a remarkable case recounted by de Waal (2001) of a dog in a zoo in Thailand, who reared three tiger cubs along with her own puppy, and the five animals continued to share a cage when the tigers were fully grown). Family pets are often known to take special care of the children and to accept ill-treatment from a child that they would never tolerate from an adult. A more dramatic incident occurred when a three-year-old boy fell into the gorilla enclosure at Brookfield Zoo in Chicago and lay unconscious on the concrete floor; a female gorilla rescued him and took him to safety (de Waal, 2001). Brian Masters (1996) also tells of gorillas taking care of young humans, showing a remarkable degree of sensitivity to their vulnerability. Animals also care for adults of other species if they are injured or otherwise vulnerable. There are stories of humans being protected from sharks by a pod of dolphins, for example.

Humans display similar emotions, showing a caring disposition towards the young of other species. People commonly have special feelings towards young animals. Konrad Lorenz (1954) tells of how he was accustomed to feeding snakes with dead mice — and he had no compunction about killing the adult mice. When the laboratory ran out of mice and he had to kill young rats in the same way, however, the experience played on his conscience and caused him much anguish.

This care for young and vulnerable members of other species seems to be contrary to natural selection, but it can be seen as an example of the principle set out on page 34: that the habit of caring for one's own young is a product of natural selection, and once the habit is part of an animal's nature it is expressed in other ways as well. It is quite common for other animals to extend this habit of caring to young and vulnerable members of other species, but no other animals extend it as widely as humans do.

Cooperation and Reciprocal Altruism

Cooperation is intended to bring benefits to all participants. Altruism (page 27) is intended to be a one-way process. As we saw on page 35, evolutionary correctness has a particular problem with morality. Thus Edward O Wilson wrote in *Sociobiology* (1975) that the central theoretical problem of sociobiology was 'how can altruism ... evolve by natural selection?' 'The answer', he continued, 'is kinship.' Care for the young and other kin can enable the altruist's genes to be perpetuated, and can thus be explained by natural selection, but there remains a difficulty where the beneficiary is not related to the altruist. To solve this problem, Robert Trivers (1971) developed a model of reciprocal altruism to show how, in certain conditions, altruistic behaviour towards non-kin can benefit the altruist and be selected by natural selection.

Human beings are gregarious, and human life is based on a great deal of cooperation. This is based on practical self-interest and is also supported by moral principle. The moral basis for reciprocal altruism is expressed in the saying that 'one good turn deserves another'. We often feel that favours should be repaid, and that this is a moral issue. Cooperation can be seen as part of our inheritance from our pre-human ancestors: cooperation in chimpanzees, for example, includes food sharing, collaborative hunting and dominance alliances (e.g. de Waal, 1996).

The economy

The basic human economy is an example of cooperation. At its heart lie mutuality and reciprocity. It is a system based on division of labour, free trade and market forces — in which sales, purchases, employment and contracts all take place by mutual agreement and everyone is free to enter into agreements and free not to. It is a system that develops naturally; it is not imposed from outside. At its best, such a free-market economy works to everyone's benefit. Customers, providers, employers and employees only receive what they require if they also deliver their part of the bargain, and this ensures that the principles of fair dealing are upheld. Thus Peter Vardy, in *Business Morality* (1989), proposes as a general principle in business, 'People matter, they are important, treat others as you expect to be treated.'

When we make a purchase, for example, or take a job we are furthering our own interests — but we are also furthering the interests of the other party to the deal. Simple self-interest thus lies at the heart of the free market. It is the driving force behind it, but, as Amartya Sen (1999) points out, the success of the capitalist economy is also dependent on 'powerful systems of values and norms. Indeed, to see capitalism as nothing other than a system based on a conglomeration of greedy behaviour is to underestimate vastly the ethics of capitalism, which has richly contributed to its redoubtable achievements.'

Sen goes on to say that the weakness of capitalist ethics lies, in part, in its failure to deal with the issues of economic inequality and environmental protection. A free market exists to benefit those who freely put something into it, and it thus has nothing to offer, directly, to the destitute, if they have no bargaining power and nothing to contribute in return, nor to the environment or posterity. However, it has the flexibility to adapt to what its contributors/consumers ask of it.

A concern about economic inequality is a moral concern, and it can readily be integrated into a thriving free-market economy. The richer we are, the more we pay in taxes. We can make charitable donations with the wealth generated by a successful economy. Many of our individual choices in the free market may be based on moral considerations. We may decide to buy fairly traded food, to benefit people in poorer countries, for example, or we may buy locally grown food, to benefit local producers. We may choose a job because of the opportunities it gives us to help other people. The economy and society in general are greatly helped by people who do voluntary work, or in some other way contribute more to society than they are paid for: there is a strong link between the amount of voluntary work in a community and the level of life satisfaction (study by Essex University; *Daily Telegraph*, 21 September 2004).

Similarly with environmental protection (see page 76), if we, as individuals, decide to make purchases that are in the interests of long-term sustainability, the market will respond. If we all demand goods that will last, that are energy-efficient and that were produced with the minimum of pollution, that is what producers will offer. If we demand less energy, less will be produced.

At its best, then, free-market capitalism is a sound basis for an economy. At its worst, however, it can enable the strong to impose their own terms on the weak, and the latter have no choice but to accept: this is where a modern government may intervene and regulate the economy.

Cooperation in modern human societies and modern economies goes far beyond the cooperative hunting parties of other animals. Our inherited instincts for cooperation may be sufficient to make the free market work in small communities, but in larger communities, where people don't all know each other, these instincts need the support of intelligent, moral thinking. We depend on other people, many of whom we do not know personally, and we count on them to carry out their functions in the way that we expect. We have to trust one another, and trust is a moral issue. The widespread denial of the moral dimension during the twentieth century (see Chapter 2, particularly, page 21) may be partly responsible for recent failures in the capitalist economy. Adam Smith, the 'father of modern economics', recognised the importance of the moral dimension in economics, but we have sometimes lost sight of this in recent years. The view that the sole responsibility of company managers is to their shareholders, for example, can lead to disaster if we do not also recognise the importance of satisfied customers, a motivated workforce and the respect of the community. Robert McGarvey (2005) writes that 'during the 1990s deception and fraud had in some sense become established norms in the upper echelons of corporate America. In the interests of maintaining a free and liberal economy perhaps we should be re-examining some of these "customs".' He goes on to call for a review of the ethical foundation of free-market capitalism.

Most people behave conscientiously, and most of our daily dealings with other people are characterised by friendliness and trust. We can usually take this for granted, but from time to time people let us down. There is a role for the law here in setting standards of behaviour. In recent years we have found that our dealings with one another, in the public and private sectors, have been regulated more and more by law and by codes of practice. While this has obvious advantages, there are also drawbacks (see, for example, Vardy, 1989; O'Neill, 2002). The new legal requirements may be less stringent and certainly less flexible than the strict but unwritten moral codes that they replace. By discouraging, or even preventing, us from using our own professional and moral judgement, they are inhibiting us from serving our public to the best of our ability. The publicity given to wrongdoing and to the supposed need for additional government intervention encourages us to believe that we cannot trust each other, and a climate of institutional distrust thus comes into being. When we fear that we are not trusted, we may lose confidence in our own judgement and, instead, work merely to externally imposed rules and guidelines.

Government interference, bureaucratic constraints and regulation from the centre make a very poor substitute for cooperation, interdependence, mutual respect, trust and goodwill — underpinned by a recognition that morality matters. It is only the reinstatement of a respect for moral thinking and moral behaviour in our economy, our institutions and society as a whole that can save us from an ever-increasing burden of legislation, rules and bureaucratic control, with the inflexibility, insensitivity and economic inefficiency that they entail.

Retaliation versus Conflict Avoidance

How do humans and other animals react when hurt by a member of the same species? Retaliation is an important principle in human behaviour, but perhaps not as universally powerful as we might think. The principle of an equal response for injury ('tit for tat'; 'an eye for an eye, and a tooth for a tooth') is widely understood. When we have been hurt, the wish to get even is strong. Then, in order to be quite sure that the reaction is sufficient, we may retaliate with a reaction which is rather greater than the original action; this, in turn, can lead to a more-than-sufficient response — and a minor dispute escalates into a larger one. Thus some feuds, between individuals and between communities, continue for a very long time.

However, these long-running feuds seem like tragic curiosities (e.g. the Montagues and Capulets in *Romeo and Juliet*). They are unusual, and that is what makes them noteworthy and newsworthy. They invite attention because they do not represent normal behaviour. Most individuals and most communities prefer peace and reconciliation ('let bygones be bygones'; 'time is a great healer'; 'a lot of water has flowed under the bridge'). The wish to be at peace and avoid conflict usually wins in the end. Jean Piaget, in his classic study *The Moral Judgment of the Child*, first published in England in 1932, found that children begin by simply practising reciprocity and later come to set forgiveness above revenge. He quotes a boy aged ten who explained this, not by lofty moral idealism, but with the more pragmatic reason that 'there is no end' to revenge.

Retaliation is a natural response in other animals (it is common for an animal that has been attacked by a member of the same species to fight back — and this includes delayed revenge), but so is the wish to keep conflict within limits and avoid it becoming excessively destructive (e.g. de Waal, 1989, 1996, 2001; Flack and de Waal, 2000). Lorenz (1952, 1966) has shown that animals such as wolves, which have the ability and opportunity to kill members of the same species, have strong instinctive restraints. In a fight between two wolves, for example, when one has established his dominance the loser bares his neck to the victor in surrender — and the victor, ruled by a powerful instinctive inhibition, is unable to attack the proffered throat. 'A wolf', wrote Lorenz (1952), 'has enlightened me: not so your enemy may strike you again do you turn the other cheek toward him, but to make him unable to do it.'

Thus, retaliation and conflict avoidance are instincts that humans share with other animals. In humans, they are seen in people of strong moral principle and in people who are not so strongly motivated by morality. It seems very likely, therefore, that these behaviour patterns are inherited from our pre-human ancestors. If this is so, when humans acquired a moral sense, it became associated both with the principle of retaliation and with that of peace-seeking. Both principles have a part in political and social thinking. In the minor conflicts of day-to-day life, however, we are more apt to make a moral principle out of retaliation. Conflict avoidance and peace-seeking come naturally to us, and we just get on with them without making a moral issue of it.

War

War is not murder (which is discussed below). War seems to be rare in animals, only occurring in social insects, dolphins, chimpanzees and humans — all of which are social creatures. Jane Goodall (1990) describes warfare among chimpanzees in the wild. Young adult males clearly find inter-group conflict attractive, in spite of the danger: 'If young male pre-humans also found excitement in encounters of this sort, this would have provided a firm biological basis for the glorification of warriors and warfare.'

As with retaliation and conflict avoidance, the human moral sense sends out conflicting messages, both of them quite powerful. On the one hand, it tells us that it is a noble thing to fight for our country — or for our gang. Comparison with Goodall's chimpanzees suggests that this may be another example of the moral sense endorsing inherited instinctive behaviour. On the other hand, when we take a more detached view, we regard war as bad. War should be avoided wherever possible, and should only be fought where necessary. These two moral positions manage to coexist. We deplore warfare. We express regret about the wars of the past, and it is our policy to avoid wars in the future. But when we are at war, we admire those who fight and risk their lives for their country. There are few situations that bring out the selfless, self-giving, self-sacrificing side of human nature so strongly as war, and we honour those who fight and die for their country.

To Augustine, who lived from 354 to 430 and played a significant part in developing a Christian ethic of the just war, the real evil of war was not the death of people who would soon die anyway, but rather the love of violence, revenge, cruelty and lust of power that accompanied it (Goddard, 2003). Today, we cannot treat loss of life so lightly. Improvements in medicine have led to an increase in life expectancy, and this is accompanied by a greater sense of the value of each individual life. A further factor is the advent of television, so that the suffering of war and the numbers of casualties, which were previously hidden from the civilian population, are brought home to people with a greater immediacy than before. These developments have led us to place greater value on the lives of military personnel. The invention and development of the aeroplane and the rocket enabled us to bomb targets from a safe distance, protecting military personnel but exposing civilians to greater risk. At the beginning of the twentieth century the ratio of military to civilian casualties was 8 to 1. By the end of the century it was 1 to 8 (Smith, 2001). This involvement of the civilian population marks a very significant change in the nature of warfare. There is a nobility about a volunteer army who regard their cause as one worth dying for. It is less easy to see nobility in the kind of war where most of the casualties are non-combatants.

The Ten Commandments

The Ten Commandments form an important part of the moral tradition of Judaism and Christianity. Four of them relate to patterns of behaviour that we observe in other animals.

Respect for life ('You shall not murder')

In modern Western society, murder is fairly unusual. The instinctive constraints are strong, and temptation is seldom strong enough to overcome them. Thus, murder would be unusual even without the added constraint of moral considerations. However, conscience reinforces the instinctive constraints and can help to prevent murder when temptation is strong.

It seems reasonable to suggest that our pre-moral ancestors likewise had strong instinctive constraints, so that intra-specific killing was rare, as it is for other social animals (e.g. Lorenz 1952, 1966). Among chimpanzees, life-threatening attacks are less common within communities than between them (war): aggressive behaviour is common within communities, but it very rarely results in death (Goodall, 1990; de Waal, 1989, 1996).

Respect for marriage ('You shall not commit adultery')

When we look at marriage systems and sexual behaviour we find a different picture. Moral feelings are very strong (so much so that in common parlance the word 'morality' is often taken to mean 'sexual morality'), but they mostly relate to custom rather than to universal human values. In this respect, they differ from moral feelings relating to murder, for example, or cruelty, theft, truthfulness, kindness or fairness. In all of these there is general agreement about the principle, though there may be disagreement about the circumstances in which exceptions should be made — but when it comes to marriage and sexual behaviour there are serious moral debates with widely differing points of view over matters of principle. All that we can agree on is that there should be some kind of moral regulation of sexual conduct, and that this regulation should include avoidance of incest (Brown's (1991) list of *Human Universals* includes sexual regulation, sexual jealousy and prevention or avoidance of incest).

The norms of sexual practice and mating systems vary widely within the animal kingdom. Even among the apes, our closest relatives, there is no uniformity. Gibbons are monogamous. Gorillas are polygamous. Chimpanzees and bonobos have multi-male-multi-female mating systems. The hierarchy of male dominance is an important characteristic of chimpanzee society, and the higher-ranking males tend to get more opportunities to mate. Bonobos, in spite of their similarity to chimpanzees (they are a different species in the same genus), differ in their behaviour and in their social relationships. Bonobo societies are female-dominant, for example, and bonobos are noted for their unrestrained sexual behaviour (though jealousy does impose some constraints). All of these species, like humans, are gregarious. The other ape, the orang-utan, is non-gregarious, with a mating system which is thought to be intermediate between the polygamy of the gorilla and the multi-male-multi-female system of chimpanzees and bonobos (Dixon, 1998; Goodall, 1990; de Waal, 1982, 1989, 1997, 2001).

In view of this variety, we cannot look to the apes to help us to understand human patterns of sexual behaviour, let alone sexual morality. If we look at the diversity of human behaviour and aspirations we can, perhaps, see that human nature contains something of the gibbon, something of the gorilla, something of the chimp and something of the bonobo. The only inherited instinct, perhaps, is the avoidance of incest, which is common to primates and widespread throughout the animal kingdom — and this is another example of an inherited instinct that has acquired a moral dimension in humans.

That is as far as we can take it. Mating behaviour is one of the most important aspects of human behaviour, as it is for all but the simplest, asexual, animals, so I thought that sexual morality was bound to find a place in this chapter — but I was wrong. Human sexual behaviour (with the exception of incest avoidance) is not regulated by instinct but by custom, and the moral sense engages with our customs. We shall therefore return to the subject in Section 3-2.

Respect for property ('You shall not steal')

Other animals regard property as important — territory and food in particular. Ownership is settled by strength (e.g. dominance, pecking order). Territory, once acquired, is defended against competition.

It is likely, therefore, that without a moral sense humans would defend their property and would expect others to do the same, so this is another instance where the moral sense largely reinforces instinct. Humans differ from others in that, for them, relative strength does not always rest on physical strength, tested and established by a fight or scuffle, but may be established on the basis of intelligence, force of personality, the ability to form powerful alliances (alliances are important in establishing dominance in other primates, too) or some other mental attribute.

Respect for the truth
('You shall not bear false witness against your neighbour')

Humans are more deceitful than any other animal. Calculated deception is quite common in humans, occasional in chimpanzees, and rather rare in other animals. Lorenz (1954) gives examples for dogs.

It is important to see human deceitfulness in perspective, however. Respect for truth is universal. Speech and language are underpinned by the concept of truth. The point has been well made by Bertrand Russell (1940):

> There is, however, a difference between the effectiveness of a lie and that of the truth: a lie only produces the desired result so long as the truth is expected. In fact, no one could learn to speak unless truth were the rule: if, when your child sees a dog, you say 'cat', 'horse', or 'crocodile', at random, you will not be able to deceive him by saying 'dog' when it is not a dog. Lying is thus a derivative activity, which presupposes truth-speaking as the usual rule.

It is interesting, in this context, to note that Charles Darwin (1874) remarked that a love of truth was one of the virtues prized by some of the peoples he referred to as 'savage tribes'.

This respect for truth has deep roots. Communication in animals is founded on truth. If their actions or the sounds they make are intended to convey information, their message is, with rare exceptions, truthful. This is the human inheritance. When humans acquired a moral sense, truth-telling was another of the activities to acquire a moral dimension. This would only have occurred, though, when deceit became a real possibility: where there is no choice, there is no moral principle.

It is noteworthy that the only species with a moral sense — which includes the moral principle that truth-telling is good and deceit is bad — is the species most prone to deceitful behaviour. This is a good example of the general principle that, as a control on behaviour, the moral sense is less effective than instinct.

It's Not Fair!

A sense of fairness is an important part of our moral sense. Children soon learn the cry, 'It's not fair'. We feel that it is right that we should be fair in our dealings with other people. We are morally disturbed by actions and situations that we feel are unfair, and we criticise them on moral grounds. We may be uncomfortable about receiving generosity that we think is undeserved, or accepting an arrangement that we feel favours us unfairly.

And yet, life is not fair. The world is not fair. Natural selection is not fair. It is fundamental to the nature of creation that it is not fair. It could not be otherwise. Our sense of fairness is not based on rational thought. Rational thought leads to the conclusion that unfairness is inevitable. We would not really ask for a world in which everybody had the same amount of happiness and suffering, and everybody died at the same age. Nor could we define how much unfairness was acceptable — set a point at which we can say 'so far, but no further'. However, rational arguments like this do not stop us feeling a sense of moral indignation when we think that someone has been unfairly treated by circumstances.

The sense of fairness is not derived from emotion either. Emotions lead us to want the best for the people we know and like best. We don't have the same emotions towards those whom we dislike, those who have hurt us, those who threaten us in one way or another; we may even feel rather pleased when they suffer some undeserved misfortune — but our sense of fairness makes us feel guilty at being pleased.

The sense of fairness runs contrary to the grain of creation. The Bible teaches that God is not fair. The book of Job tells the story of a man who suffered great misfortune — wholly undeserved, as he was a God-fearing man of the greatest integrity. We read of attempts by Job and his friends to explain his suffering, and finally we read of God's response. Believers will heed the arguments, but our sense that Job and his family were unfairly treated remains with us — and this is a moral sense.

In the New Testament, the story of the workers in the vineyard (Matthew 20:1–15) tells how the same pay was given to each man at the end of the day, regardless of how many hours he had worked. Those who had worked through the heat of the day received the pay that had been agreed before they started work, but they protested that it was unfair that those who had done less work received the same pay. The purpose of this story is to illustrate the boundless grace of God on a scale that makes any protest of 'It's not fair' seem rather petty. As with the story of Job, Christians may accept the teaching — but the sense of unfairness remains.

The question of fairness is bound up with the problem of suffering. Suffering and early death offend against our sense what is right, and we ask why God allows it. Even if we accept the rational basis for the answers (e.g. C S Lewis's *The Problem of Pain*) we still find it difficult to accept the apparently haphazard way in which suffering is dealt out.

Humans thus have a deep-seated sense of fairness, for which there is no obvious explanation in terms of reason, emotion, or God. The sense of fairness is widely shared (it is a human universal; Brown, 1991), and does not give rise to much moral debate or disagreement. This suggests the possibility that it might have its origins in our inheritance from our pre-human ancestors, and recent experimental studies with brown capuchin monkeys, published by Sarah Brosnan and Frans de Waal in the journal *Nature*, provide evidence that this might be so.

Pairs of these monkeys were trained to hand tokens to human researchers in exchange for food. At first, both monkeys were always given the same reward, a piece of cucumber. They were happy with this arrangement: in 95 per cent of cases, the animals handed over their tokens and happily took and ate the cucumber. In the next stage, however, the monkeys were treated differently. One was given a piece of cucumber, as before, but the other was given a sweet and juicy grape. The monkeys' reaction was most interesting. Monkeys that had previously been quite happy with a slice of cucumber stopped accepting it when they saw their partners getting a grape. Some went on strike, refusing to swap any more tokens, while others took the cucumber but wouldn't eat it. Some threw outright tantrums, throwing the cucumber out of the cage. Only 60 per cent of the animals now would exchange a token for cucumber in the normal way. If one of the monkeys was rewarded for doing nothing, its partner's behaviour became even worse. This was considered such an insult that 80 per cent of the monkeys refused to take any further part in the test.

This story with monkeys as the players is strikingly similar to the Bible story of the workers in the vineyard and to human nature as we know it. It would be going too far to say that the monkeys were displaying a sense of fairness, because this would require a degree of mental detachment that is beyond the reach of the monkey mind. In the experiment, it was only the aggrieved monkeys who showed their displeasure; in fair-minded humans the indignation would also be felt by onlookers and by those favoured with a grape. Brosnan and de Waal use the term 'inequity aversion', but perhaps 'envy' would also describe the feelings of the monkeys. Nevertheless, if strong feelings of envy at such treatment are part of our inheritance from our pre-human primate ancestors, they could develop into a sense of fairness when the human mind became capable of sympathising with anyone fobbed off with a mere cucumber, and this combination of feelings could readily be incorporated into a human sense of right and wrong. This could account for the moral sense of fairness, which, as we have seen, is otherwise rather difficult to understand.

Guilt

If we think we have behaved in a way that does not conform to our moral values, we feel guilty. Our self-image is damaged, and we are uncomfortable. We can learn from the experience and avoid similar feelings of guilt in the future by changing our behaviour. For the present, though, we have to face up to the damage to our self-image and do our best to repair it. We can do that by apology and confession. If our behaviour has caused hurt to another, we can apologise, we can make amends in some other way, and we can accept punishment. Alternatively, we can try to deny the event, or justify or excuse our behaviour, or revise our moral values ('It doesn't *really* matter'), or persuade ourselves that the victim actually deserved the pain the we have caused, or even try to block out the memory of what we have done (see Derek Wright's *The Psychology of Moral Behaviour*, which has a chapter devoted to 'reactions to transgression').

Guilt can be damaging. It can cause considerable unhappiness. Bertrand Russell (1930) regarded the sense of sin as one of the most important of the underlying psychological causes of unhappiness in adult life. It can damage the personality and give rise to physical illness. Psychiatrists recognise the condition of pathological guilt — guilt that does not appear to be justified by actual transgression and that is not readily alleviated (Wright, 1971). From his experience as a therapist, Malan (1995), after remarking on the role of guilt and concern for others in influencing our behaviour, concludes that 'we should thank our Maker or evolution (or both) for *concern*, but I do not feel inclined to offer any thanks for *guilt*, which is a force too powerful, too lasting, too destructive and in the end often ineffective, as we discover time and again in psychotherapy.'

Guilt can also be complicated. Doing what we know to be right cannot be guaranteed to dispel guilty feelings. When different moral principles or arguments lead to different conclusions, any decision will be contrary to one or the other. If, for example, loyalty to a friend requires you to be dishonest, you cannot avoid being either dishonest or disloyal — and you may feel guilty as a result. Moral thinking and moral planning can assess moral values, where they are in conflict, and reach a conclusion. Guilt shows no such rationality: if one moral principle or argument is sacrificed for another, guilt can result. A book for working mothers trying to balance career and family life (Gillibrand and Mosley, 1997) is entitled *When I go to work I feel guilty*, evoking the image of a woman making what she judges to be the morally right decision — but still feeling guilty. The wish to avoid feeling guilty cannot therefore be the only reason for moral behaviour. We still wish to seek the most moral way forward, even when we know that whichever decision we make we are still likely to experience feelings of guilt.

Do other animals experience guilt? Any dog owner will be familiar with an expression and behaviour which, in humans, would be interpreted as guilt: fear of retribution, combined with submissiveness. They seem to understand unquestioning obedience and they fear the consequences of disobedience. Lorenz (1954) and de Waal (1996) describe this behaviour in dogs and other animals, and both of them conclude that it is actually fear and the expectation of punishment, not guilt, that the animal experiences. Personality assessments of dogs show that they possess similar measurable personality differences to those of humans — but with the exception of conscientiousness (Gosling and others, 2003). Wright (1971) points out that there is more to guilt than just fear: 'The central point about guilt is that it is not an anxiety about some future event, but a disagreeable emotional condition which directly follows transgression'. Other animals cannot experience these sentiments, but their fear is, perhaps, a precursor of human guilt.

Fear, or anxiety, is one of the ingredients of human guilt (as Wright acknowledges), along with regret — sometimes to the extent of wishing we could turn the clock back — and anger. When we feel guilty about something, we often fear what someone else might think or do as a consequence. Sometimes we have good reason for this fear when somebody has reasonable cause to be angry with us. At other times, however, we may suffer from misplaced guilty fears. Sometimes this may be internally generated: typically, perhaps, a fear that a parent will be seriously displeased — a fear that, knowing the parent as we do, we could have known would be groundless. On other occasions, the reverse may happen: we can be made to feel guilty by the way someone reacts to something we have done that we had not thought to be wrong.

Guilt is sometimes associated with the unintended consequences of an action rather than with the action itself. Simon Blackburn (2001) gives the example of two motorists who drive along the same stretch of road at different times, each with the same small degree of careless inattention; one, because of carelessness, kills a child who runs into the road, whereas the other completes the journey without incident. Both are culpable of inattention. It is circumstances beyond the control of either motorist that leads to the consequences of their inattention being so different, but the former experiences far more guilt (and possibly a severe sentence from the criminal court). We could add a third driver on the same stretch of road, who killed a child even though his driving was impeccable. He was in no way held responsible for the accident, but nevertheless is likely to experience a sense of guilt — another example of the unreasonableness of guilt. A rather similar phenomenon is the guilt experienced by survivors from a tragedy in which other people died: entirely unreasonable, but very real to those who suffer from it.

De Waal (1996) describes misplaced guilt-like behaviour in dogs. In one example the animal was wholly blameless and in the other (from Lorenz, 1954) the distress was vastly excessive and the dog would not be comforted.

If we try to disentangle our moral sense from these feelings of fear that are our inheritance, what might we find? If, for the sake of argument, we accept (1) that humans are moral beings, wanting to lead moral lives and (2) that we are rational beings, able to think problems through to a rational conclusion, how might we expect that we would behave when we know that we have done wrong? First, I suggest, we would accept and come to terms with the fact of our wrongdoing. Secondly, we would experience genuine regret (penitence), appropriate to the nature of the transgression. Thirdly, we would see if there was anything we could do to put the situation right: an apology, if anyone was hurt, and any restitution, repayment or reparation that was appropriate. Fourthly, we would accept any punishment that was appropriate. Finally, we would learn from our error and avoid repeating it.

If we compare this moral and rational response to wrongdoing with the kind of behaviour and thought processes associated with guilt, what do we find? First, the pain and fear associated with guilt can make us disinclined to come to terms with the realities of the situation; we may be more inclined to deny our wrongdoing, or seek excuses, or try to justify ourselves, or tell ourselves that it was all the other person's fault anyway. Secondly, guilt mixes regret with fear, and may be disproportionate to the nature of the transgression. Thirdly, if we cannot come to terms with the reality of the situation, we may not be able to bring ourselves to make appropriate apology and restitution.

Bertrand Russell (1930) goes so far as to argue that the sense of sin does not necessarily make us better, more moral people:

> As a matter of fact, the sense of sin, so far from being a cause of a good life, is quite the reverse. It makes a man unhappy and it makes him feel inferior. Being unhappy, he is likely to make claims upon other people which are excessive and which prevent him from enjoying happiness in personal relations. Feeling inferior, he will have a grudge against those who seem superior. He will find admiration difficult and envy easy. He will become a generally disagreeable person …

According to Derek Wright (1971), it is indeed the case that guilt does not correlate with leading a moral life: there is evidence that the kind of upbringing that predisposes children to guilt is different from that which helps them to acquire the ability to resist temptation. Similarly, Buddhists regard unhealthy fears arising from wrongdoing as obstructions to the leading of a morally good life; guilt is not a concept that fits into the Buddhist analysis of wrongdoing (de Silva, 1991).

Wright, Russell and other writers have emphasised the importance of early upbringing in making people predisposed to guilt, and this is undoubtedly a powerful influence. However, human nature is not a blank slate (Pinker, 2002), and I suggest that some of the manifestations of guilt owe much to the fear of punishment that is part of our animal inheritance. This inheritance includes the fear of an authority figure, and it may be this that makes children so susceptible to guilt. Most of our childhood fears we can easily grow out of, but it seems that guilt is not one of them; our animal inheritance could provide an explanation. Anthony Stevens and John Price (1966; and Stevens, 1998) have suggested that an evolutionary perspective can help to explain certain psychiatric conditions. Pathological guilt may be an example of this.

To conclude, then, feelings of guilt — and the wish to avoid guilt — can encourage us to live moral lives, but guilt is often misdirected and ineffective at encouraging moral behaviour. The reasons for this are partly the fear that is attached to guilt and partly its failure to correlate with a realistic sense of what is right and wrong.

Conclusion: Good Behaviour, Bad Behaviour and the Moral Sense in an Evolutionary Perspective

The behaviour and thinking we have looked at in this section relate to issues that humans regard as moral issues; but they also resemble behaviour seen in other species, animals with no capacity to make moral judgements. The behaviour patterns themselves, in other animals and to a considerable extent in ourselves, are motivated and regulated by instinct.

We have looked at patterns of behaviour that are essential to the life of a chimpanzee community, for example, and which, in humans, are supported by the moral sense. Not all such patterns are endorsed by the moral sense, however. To take one example, chimpanzee societies are hierarchical. The top-ranking male (alpha male) is dominant, and there is a hierarchy based on strength (a combination of physical strength and personality). This is an integral part of the way that chimpanzee society works: a product, no doubt, of natural selection. Some kind of power and dominance is essential for the smooth running of human communities, too (total anarchy offers no protection for the weak), but, increasingly, it comes into conflict with our moral sense.

De Waal (2001) combines Westermarck's (1912) writings on morality with his own observations as a primatologist to emphasise the similarities between humans and other primates in what might be called 'good' behaviour:

> When I watch primates, measuring how they share food in return for grooming, comfort victims of aggression, or wait for the right opportunity to get even with a rival, I see very much the same emotional impulses that Westermarck analysed. A group of chimpanzees, for example, may whip up an outraged chorus of barks when the dominant male overdoes his punishment of an underling, and in the wild they form cooperative hunting parties that share the spoils of their efforts. Although I shy away from calling chimpanzees 'moral beings', their psychology contains many of the ingredients that, if also present in the progenitor of humans and apes, must have allowed our ancestors to develop a moral sense. Instead of seeing morality as a radically new invention, I tend to view it as a natural outgrowth of ancient social tendencies.

He goes on say that Westermarck considered 'disinterestedness' to be a characteristic of moral feelings. For all the similarity of behaviour and emotional impulse, this disinterestedness, or detachment, is a characteristic of human thinking that is different from anything seen in other primates. Thus, other animals show unquestioning obedience to authority (i.e. strength or dominance), but only humans have the independence of mind to be able to challenge authority on moral grounds. To de Waal, primate behaviour that is similar to human moral behaviour suggests emotions that are similar to human emotions, and this leads him to conclude that morality is a 'natural outgrowth' from these emotions. However, it would be possible to use the same evidence to reach a different conclusion: that these patterns of behaviour and their accompanying emotions are so well developed and work so effectively in animals without a moral sense that the moral dimension is an unnecessary irrelevance. 'Behaviours that people do spontaneously by virtue of their own desires don't need to have a moral code laid on top of them' (Sober and Wilson, 2000). Whether the moral sense was a 'new invention' or a 'natural outgrowth', however, the evidence we have been looking at does support de Waal's point that the psychology of our pre-human ancestors was ready to receive the moral sense.

Animals also exhibit behaviour that, in a human, we would say was morally wrong. Robert Sapolsky (2001) describes the baboons of the Serengeti as working for maybe four hours a day for food, leaving them 'about a half dozen solid hours of sunlight a day to devote to being rotten to each other. Just like our society …' Chimpanzees (e.g. Goodall, 1990) can share their food — but they can also steal food from one another. They can show kindness — but they can also pursue their own ends with scant regard for others: struggles for dominance can lead to serious injury, for example. Animals can care for young that are not their own offspring, as we have seen, but they can also prey on eggs and young animals of their own species: a nesting herring gull will eat another herring gull's eggs if left unguarded (Tinbergen, 1953); a black-headed gull will eat a chick from another black-headed gull's nest, given the opportunity (Dawkins, 1976); and at Gombe a chimpanzee mother and daughter killed and ate several newborn chimpanzees in their own community (Goodall, 1990).

Humans and chimpanzees are alike in having instincts that hold them back from committing murder. They are alike in that these instinctive restraints sometimes fail and murder takes place — the murder of a rival in a struggle for power, for example. Where they differ is that when a chimpanzee murders a rival there are no moral overtones or considerations. What happens, happens. When a man does the same, however, morality clicks in: the murderer may experience temptation before the event and guilt after it, and bystanders may experience moral disapproval. Humans and other animals show a range of behaviour patterns, good and bad. Only humans have the mental detachment that enables us to discriminate between them.

Insofar as 'morality' means 'good behaviour', then, the similarity between human behaviour and that of other primates supports the view that the human 'good' behaviour and moral thinking described in this section can be understood in terms of our animal ancestry. Insofar as 'morality' refers to the possession of a moral sense, the capacity to make individual moral judgements and the capacity to recognise temptation and resist it, however, its origin remains an open question, to which we shall return in Chapter 4.

3-2. The Morality of Custom: To Conform or to Challenge

> If a man does away with his traditional way of living and throws away his good customs, he had better first make certain that he has something of value to replace them.
>
> Sotho proverb, quoted by Robert Ruark, *Something of Value*

One of the characteristics of human societies is the extent to which their behaviour is regulated by social custom — the way that people behave and think about things, differing in many important respects from other communities. I use the word 'custom' to describe conventional behaviour and thinking which have been learned from others (see page 2). Other animals develop customs (see, particularly, de Waal, 2001), but humans are unique in the importance that we attach to them in our social life and in how strongly they shape what we expect of one another.

I am suggesting that there is a useful distinction to be made between innate conventional behaviour that is found throughout the human species (often similar to the behaviour of other primate species), and conventional behaviour that has been learned and is found throughout a particular community (while other communities have different conventions). The interaction of the moral sense with innate behaviour patterns formed the basis of the previous section; its interaction with learned behaviour is considered here.

To Conform ...

There are two ways in which the moral sense engages with custom. First, it is widely regarded as morally good to conform to the customs of one's own people. As far as records go back, it seems that every community or tribe had its customs, its ceremonies and its rituals; and these customs were enforced by moral sanction. Customs provide social cohesion and a sense of belonging, and they distinguish members of one society from people belonging to another. Many day-to-day decisions are made easier if everyone knows what is expected of them. Behaviour that is governed by custom includes such vitally important activities as eating habits, marriage and family relationships, sexual behaviour, how we greet one another, the language or dialect we speak, and rituals surrounding death and bereavement, as well as the finer points of day-to-day social interaction. Some customs are positive, things that must be done; others are negative, behaviour to be avoided. As the educationalist W R Niblett wrote in 1963,

> Most people for most of their lives fit easily into the expectations of their time and place about how they should behave. ... One tends to follow the Joneses not only in matters of dress, speech and diet but more or less in standards of honesty, truth-telling, treatment of parents, sexual conduct, attitude to criminals and so on. In the eighteenth century it was good men, not only bad, who saw nothing that was wrong in owning slaves or hanging a sheep-stealer.

We can see some similarities with other social species. The behaviour of these animals is instinctive, lacking the variety of locally developed customs, but it may serve a similar purpose in creating social cohesion. Frans de Waal (1996) writes about 'a sense of social regularity', based on 'a set of expectations'. Social relationships include acknowledgement of the authority of a dominant member of the group. As with humans, a recognition of hierarchical relationships seems to give a sense of security as well as protection for the weak. Hierarchical relationships are not permanent, however, and individuals look for opportunities to improve their standing. Animals display a negative reaction when reality differs from these expectations. The importance of expectations is therefore something that human societies have in common with other species. The general sense that we should conform to expectations may, thus, be inherited from the behaviour of our pre-human ancestors, but the actual customs that we expect people to conform to are generally specific to our own people.

The moral pressures to conform are much weaker in Western society than they used to be, but we do not have to go far back in time or look far into other cultures today to find situations in which the pressures to live up to expectations and conform to conventional practice are very strong indeed. This applies to important areas of life such as the upbringing of children, sexual behaviour and marriage customs. It can also apply in areas of behaviour that might seem less important, such as clothing or eating habits. Philippa Foot's (1954) sensible argument that for a principle to be a moral principle it must be serious (she points out that a trivial rule, like 'One should never step on the lines on a pavement' cannot be regarded as a moral principle, for example) appears to break down when we look at the morality of custom, where quite trivial matters of behaviour can come to be regarded as of moral importance. We can reconcile such trivial moral rules with Foot's point if we see conformity, rather than the rule itself, as being the moral principle. There is much more freedom and tolerance in British society today, but even so, most of us, most of the time, conform to a lot of the conventional practices and opinions of those around us. We expect other people to conform, and they expect the same of us.

Children are brought up to eat with chopsticks, or knife and fork, or fingers, according to the custom of their parents and their community. That is how children 'ought' to eat, not because one type of table manners is intrinsically superior, in moral terms, to another, but because a society feels more comfortable about itself if certain customs are generally observed by all its members. If English people are dining in a Chinese restaurant in England, they may use chopsticks (conforming with the traditional way of eating Chinese food) or knife and fork (conforming to their own traditions), but to use neither and eat with their fingers would be discourteous to the staff of the restaurant and to their fellow diners — and therefore might be thought morally wrong.

If conformity is regarded as morally good, it is not surprising, perhaps, that people came to regard the individual customs of their communities as morally good in their own right — and, by implication, departures from these customs as wrong. This represents a significant departure from everything we have seen about the moral sense so far. The moral sentiments that we looked at in the last section are all shared. We may differ in how much importance to attach to each moral principle, and we may disagree about how a moral principle should be applied, but there is broad agreement about the principles and sentiments themselves. We can look at conformity to custom in the same way, as a general principle that is applied in different ways. However, once we start attaching moral values to specific customs, we lose all common ground. Customs reflect the diversity of human societies, and it can often happen that the customs of one community are directly opposed to those of another.[1] It is hardly surprising, therefore, that many of the most difficult ethical controversies are concerned with customs, and the disagreements can be particularly intractable if the conflicting views are supported by religious teaching.

As a general principle, then, it is considered to be good to conform, out of courtesy and consideration to other people in the community. What about rebels, though? Inflexible and unsympathetic enforcement of customs in the belief that this is a moral good can, in some circumstances, be regarded as morally wrong, if it makes people feel imprisoned by the social code, having to choose between suppression of their own personalities and the distress to themselves and their community of becoming rebels. Conformity need not always be stifling, though: independent spirits may benefit from outward conformity for the security it brings, freeing the mind to chart its own individual course. Freedom may flourish best in a secure and stable environment.

There is another, more important, reason why it may not seem right to regard conformity as a moral good, and that is the diversity of communities and the overlap between them. Many people, these days, belong to more than one community and feel under moral pressure to conform to more than one set of customs. If it was ever justifiable to adopt the attitude that 'my customs are right, and those of other communities are inferior and morally wrong', such an attitude raises serious problems now, with the risk of intercommunal discord. If we believe that other people's customs are morally wrong, this can lead to the belief that the people themselves are wrong, or inferior, offering a moral basis for prejudices against other classes, castes, nationalities and races. In today's world, we wish, and need, to understand other people's customs and, wherever we can, see them as just as valid as our own.

... Or to Challenge

This brings us to the second way in which morality impinges on custom: there are times when people feel that some of the customs of

---

[1]   Silberbauer (1991), for example, records that, because of the different social structures of the Tswana of Botswana and the Shona of Zimbabwe, the former regard marriage between cousins as a good and sensible practice, whereas the latter regard it as incest and therefore abhorrent. To take another example, some people in Britain today experience the conflict between a custom in which marriages are arranged and a custom in which people choose their own marriage partners.

their own community — or of another community — are morally wrong, and that the moral principle that leads them to this belief is stronger than the principle that leads them to conform.

As we look back through history and around the world, it is quite remarkable how common it is for societies to develop customs that are cruel to some of their own members: to women, perhaps, or children, or people who are weak and vulnerable. Once established, customs that are hideously cruel come to be taken for granted and remain unchallenged because of the moral pressure to conform. The strength of this force is often underestimated (Wright, 1971). William Golding's novel, *Lord of the Flies*, and Stanley Milgram's experiments[2] demonstrate chillingly how strongly, and easily, people can be influenced by the desire to retain the approval of those around them — to follow the crowd or to obey an authority figure — pressures powerful enough to overcome any other moral feelings they may have.

The cruel customs of societies can only be changed if somebody rejects conformity and starts a new way of thinking about issues. 'It is generally agreed that the higher reaches of moral development are shown precisely by those who stand out against the group in defence of their moral judgements' (Wright, 1971). 'Socrates and Jesus do not simply internalise the moral codes of their own society; they criticise them in the name of an ideal society' (Mitchell, 1969). When we use our moral judgement in this way, to question and challenge the customs and values of our own people, we can no longer find parallels in the behaviour of other animals. Instead, there is more of a similarity with the moral thinking described in the next section (pages 67–79).

Sexual Morality and Marriage Systems

On page 51 we found that human sexual behaviour was not regulated by instincts inherited from our pre-human ancestors. This lack

[2] Milgram invited volunteers to help him with an experiment to test whether the use of punishment improves the ability to learn. They were told to administer an electric shock to a 'learner' when he gave the wrong answers in a simple word-pair test. Continued wrong answers were to be met with shocks of increasing severity (from 15 volts to 450 volts), till the learner cried with pain and demanded to be set free. Contrary to what might be expected, a substantial proportion of the volunteers continued to obey instructions and administer the shocks right up to the highest level, no matter how vehemently the learner pleaded to be let out. Unknown to the volunteers, the 'learner' was in fact an actor, and there were no electric shocks: the purpose of the experiment was to ascertain how far the volunteers would go in obeying instructions (this summary is taken from Milgram, 2004; the full results of the experiment were published in 1974).

of innate patterns of sexual behaviour has enabled local customs to develop. Sexual regulation of some sort is a human universal (Brown, 1991), but the form of regulation varies between one society and another: polygamy, lifelong monogamy and serial monogamy have all been described as normative behaviour — and are granted moral approval in their communities. Sexual jealousy is also a human universal, and disapproval of unfaithfulness is widespread. Most people adopt values that conform to the customs of their group. This presents many people with a dilemma when, as in Britain today, there are different behavioural norms coexisting. It can leave them confused about a very important area of behaviour, unsure about how they should live and unsure about what they can expect of other people.

Discussion

There is probably more moral confusion about customs than about other aspects of the moral mind. The thinking described in Sections 3-1 and 3-3 can very often be related to some moral principle about which there is general agreement, but when we think about our customs we may be weighing one custom against another and we may struggle to find an agreed principle or authority to help us decide between them.

We have seen changes in our own customs, and we have seen, and learnt to accept, that other peoples have customs that differ from ours. This has led to a decline in the strength and authority of custom-based morality, and this is a trend that is likely to continue. To people who have believed that all of morality is based on custom, this has meant, inevitably, a decline in the authority of all moral teaching and the growth of moral relativism, moral doubts and moral cynicism (see Chapter 2).

We can look at any particular custom and say that, because it is only a custom it has no moral authority — but every community has *some* customs, and there is a need for them. For example, different communities have different customs and rituals for dealing with death. No one set of customs carries absolute moral authority, but if a community decided, for this reason, to do away with all customs at the time of death it would not be catering adequately for the needs of the bereaved. Again, we can ridicule chopsticks, or knife and fork, or eating with the hands, but the human head isn't well designed for eating grains of rice without some assistance. There have been countless theories about how best to bring up children, and probably most of them work best when there is broad agreement between parents, school and the local community. Every system of regulating sexual behaviour may have its faults, but most people know that they benefit from the security and trust that can only be enjoyed if there are some agreed codes of behaviour; moreover, some of our strongest moral instincts require us to provide a stable and secure environment for children to grow up in.

The Greek historian Herodotus, quoted by Blackburn (2001), felt it was right that everyone should respect their own customs. He thought this was so obvious that only a madman would mock these traditions.

Many customs are good, and valuable to society. The current relaxation of the moral sanctions that have traditionally been attached to them does not mean that the customs themselves should be abandoned. Indeed, it is possible that, freed from stifling moral sanction, people will find it easier to enjoy and celebrate the best of their traditional customs. We need the sense of belonging that communities provide, the sense that every individual has a role and a value. The knowledge that we belong to very large groups is necessary in the modern world, but it can lead to a sense of powerlessness and alienation unless it is balanced by membership of small groups — and shared customs are important in holding such communities together.

3-3. The Morality of Beyond: Reaching Out

[E]ach human being is possessed of a rationality which means that he or she can transcend what is given in biology and culture. We are prisoners neither of our genes nor of the ideas we encounter as we each make our personal and individual way through life.

Anthony O'Hear, *Beyond Evolution*

In Section 3-1 we looked at examples of moral thinking that reinforce instinctive patterns of behaviour and thought — patterns inherited from our pre-human, pre-moral ancestors. In Section 3-2 we saw how the moral sense engages with human customs. In this section we go on to see how our moral thinking goes beyond instinct and custom as we seek to find our special role as human beings.

On page 34 we saw that 'caring, most especially for the young, vulnerable and needy, is what many animals do (and humans more than others), simply because it is in their nature.' We have looked at caring behaviour in Section 3-1, but humans take this caring further. Peter Singer, in *The Expanding Circle* (1981), expressed it in this way:

The circle of altruism has broadened from the family and tribe to the nation and race, and we are beginning to recognise that our obligations extend to all human beings. The process should not stop there.

... The expansion of the moral circle should ... be pushed out until it includes most animals.

In order to discuss what this expanding circle[3] might mean in practice, we shall look first at some teaching from the New Testament. I choose this partly because its teaching is an important part of our cultural tradition and partly because it demonstrates the contrast between the social aspects of the morality of beyond and the moral thinking of the previous two sections: it is interesting to note, for example, that not one of the 105 moral statements in the Sermon on the Mount encourages moral distinctions in favour of family, tribe or race (Lahti, 2004). After looking at the first part of the expanding circle ('all human beings') in this way, we shall then go on to consider our moral feelings about other animals and the natural world. Finally, the focus shifts away from the expanding circle as we look at how we see ourselves, with a discussion of personal integrity.

The New Testament

Forgiving others

Forgiveness, rather than revenge, is the Christian response to being hurt. Christian forgiveness requires a knowledge of the hurt done by another, the (instinctive) wish to retaliate, and the deliberate choice to overrule this wish. It goes beyond the inherited, instinctive conflict-avoidance behaviour described in Section 3-1.

Forgiveness has a prominent place in Christian teaching. Christians are taught that we should forgive anyone who has injured us. This can be regarded as a commandment to be kept, however difficult it is, simply because we are commanded to do so. However, it is also apparent that there are sound reasons of self-interest for forgiving people who have hurt us deeply. An inability to forgive, a festering bitterness and resentment about some serious hurt in the past, can have a harmful effect on the personality. Forgiveness enables us to leave the bitterness behind, to leave the past behind and to move on into the future. This way of looking at forgiveness is nothing to do with fairness, reciprocity or justice: the circumstances may have fully justified the bitterness and sense of injury. Equally, it is nothing to do with generosity towards the person who was the cause of the hurt. Rather, it seems to take forgiveness out of the moral arena and make it a matter of sensible self-interest, to free oneself of life-destroying resentment to enable one to live life to the full.

---

[3]　The idea of the expanding circle does not imply that humans are getting more moral. It refers, rather, to developments in moral thinking.

Caring concern for all

Jesus taught that a loving concern for other people should be extended beyond the family, beyond one's own society, beyond one's own people. When he was asked 'Who is my neighbour?' (the questioner was referring to the commandment to love one's neighbour) he replied with the story of the good Samaritan, in which a traveller was robbed and beaten, ignored by respectable men of his own people, and finally rescued and helped by a Samaritan — a representative of a despised race (Luke 10:25–37).

He pointed out that there was nothing very special about doing good to those who do good to us (i.e. reciprocal altruism): 'Even sinners love those who love them.' He taught his followers, 'Love your enemies, do good to those who hate you, bless those who curse you, pray for those who abuse you' (Luke 6:27–36). Similarly, he told them to give parties for those who could not return the hospitality: 'When you give a luncheon or a dinner, do not invite your friends or your brothers or your relatives or rich neighbours, in case they may invite you in return, and you would be repaid. But when you give a banquet, invite the poor, the crippled, the lame, and the blind' (Luke 14:12–14).

Christian teaching, then, extends altruism, kindness and concern for others beyond the confines of our close kin and those who will return our kindness — even beyond those who we perceive as vulnerable, needy or deserving. A moral obligation to give generous hospitality to strangers, without thought of repayment, is found all over the world — perhaps more conspicuously in peasant communities than in more sophisticated societies — but Christian teaching goes beyond this.

Judging others

Jesus taught his followers not to pass judgement on other people's behaviour (Matthew 7:1–5). At first sight this may seem an extraordinary command. Making some sort of a judgement on the way other people behave is so much a part of everyday life. How can we live without making some kind of assessment of other people and the way they behave? How can we develop our moral sense and learn about good and bad behaviour except by observing and learning from other people's successes and failures as well as our own? How are we to learn about our own behaviour, if we don't get some sort of feedback from other people? Not only that, but parents, teachers, police and the criminal courts see it as their duty — their moral duty — to make a judgement about behaviour so that they can rebuke and, where appropriate, punish. Parents and teachers — and all of us — also give praise when it is due, and that, too, involves making a moral judgement.

Perhaps the answer to this lies in *how* we pass judgement on other people's behaviour. It is one thing to recognise other people's faults, understanding that they, like us, are flawed and fallible human beings. It is quite another to enjoy drawing attention to them as a means of establishing our own superiority.

The gospel accounts give several examples of Jesus rebuking self-righteous attitudes (e.g. Luke 10:38–42; 18:9–14). On several occasions morally upright citizens came to him expecting him to join with them in denouncing someone who had infringed the moral code — but he never took their side (e.g. Matthew 12:1–8, 26:6–13; John 8:1–11). It is self-satisfied judgementalism that gives morality a bad name ('the self-righteous person whose sympathy and understanding for wrongdoers has largely atrophied, and who finds it intolerable that others should transgress and get away with it'; Wright, 1971). One of the dictionary definitions of the word 'moralist' is 'a person who comments on issues of right and wrong, *typically with an unfounded air of superiority*' (my italics). If being moral means being quick to find fault with others but slow to see one's own faults, it is understandable if decent people want no part in it. When Macaulay wrote 'We know no spectacle so ridiculous as the British public in one of its periodical fits of morality' he was probably not thinking of an epidemic of kindliness or an outbreak of honesty.

We can never know the power of the temptations that other people experience, nor can we know what resources of will power they can call upon to enable them to resist. It is for this reason, not because morality doesn't matter, that we are compassionate towards other people and their wrongdoing. This is where the teaching we are considering here differs from the modern aversion to moral judgements that we considered in Chapter 2 — a way of thinking that will not accept that moral values have any validity.

These points can be illustrated by quoting from one of the outstanding Christians of our time, Desmond Tutu. In his personal memoir of his experiences as chairman of South Africa's Truth and Reconciliation Commission, *No Future Without Forgiveness* (1999), he writes that he

> ... realised how each of us has this capacity for the most awful evil — all of us. None of us could predict that if we had been subjected to the same influences, the same conditioning, we would not have turned out as these perpetrators. This is not to condone or excuse

what they did. It is to be filled more and more with the compassion of God, looking on and weeping that one of His beloved had come to such a sad pass. We have to say to ourselves with deep feeling, not with a cheap pietism, 'There but for the grace of God go I.'

And, mercifully and wonderfully, as I listened to the stories of victims I marvelled at their magnanimity, that after so much suffering instead of lusting for revenge they had this extraordinary willingness to forgive. Then I thanked God that *all* of us, even I, have this remarkable capacity for good, for generosity, for magnanimity.

Theology helped us in the Truth and Reconciliation Commission to recognise that we inhabit a moral universe, that good and evil are real and that they matter.

Other moral sentiments

The teaching of the New Testament turns some of the moral principles discussed in Section 3-1 upside down. Let us look at some examples.

Family first. Jesus remained close to his mother in his adult life and was concerned for her well-being.[4] He also took close family relationships for granted in some of the stories he told.[5] Some of his teaching to his followers, however, was not 'family first'. He expected them to leave their families for the sake of the kingdom of God.[6]

Reciprocal altruism. We have seen that Jesus' teaching was that kindness and generosity should be extended to those who would not return it.

Retaliation. After quoting the Old Testament saying, 'An eye for an eye, and a tooth for a tooth' (retaliation), Jesus continued, 'But I say to you, Do not resist an evildoer. But if anyone strikes you on the right cheek, turn the other also; and if anyone wants to sue you and take your coat, give your cloak as well' (Matthew 5:38–41).

Conflict avoidance. Throughout his ministry, Jesus had no hesitation in standing up for what was right, even though this brought him the hostility of powerful and influential people and led, ultimately, to his death.

Fairness. We have already noted that the strong human sense of fairness is at variance with New Testament teaching. Jesus' teaching is for loving concern and generosity to all, with no consideration for fairness or just deserts. In spite of this teaching, the sense of fairness still forms an important part of the moral make-up of most Christians.

---

[4]   The wedding at Cana (John 2:1–11); asking John to take care of his mother after his death (John 19:25–27).

[5]   E.g. the parables of the prodigal son (Luke 15:11–31), the rich man and Lazarus (Luke 16:19–31) and the tenants (Luke 20:9–16).

[6]   Luke 18:29–30; also Matthew 12:46–50.

The Cruel Creator?

The principal role of the moral sense, I would like to think, is to provide us with guidance as we live our lives. However, we also use it in making moral judgements about the way other people behave. This is extended into passing judgement on the way animals behave ('good dog!'; 'bad dog!') and even into passing judgement on God.

It has long been recognised that there is a problem in reconciling the existence of suffering and evil in the world with belief in the creator as all-powerful and at the same time as good and loving, in a way that the human mind understands power, goodness and love. Some people see this as an obstacle to belief in a divine creator — testimony indeed to the power of the moral sense.

There is a great deal in the natural creation that offends against our moral sense. First, there is the human suffering resulting from famine, disease and natural disaster (I am not here including suffering caused by humans themselves). Then there is cruelty inflicted by one animal on another. Carnivores killing for food, for example, or just for amusement; or the wasp that lays its eggs in a caterpillar so that its grubs can feed off the flesh of the living caterpillar.

Perhaps we have become more sensitive to suffering in animals in recent years, but a well-known passage in the Old Testament, written some 2700 years ago, conveys the sense that in God's perfect world one animal would not harm another:

> The wolf shall live with the lamb,
>   the leopard shall lie down with the kid,
> the calf and the lion and the fatling together,
>   and a little child shall lead them.
> The cow and the bear shall graze,
>   their young shall lie down together;
>   and the lion shall eat straw like the ox.
> The nursing child shall play over the hole of the asp,
>   and the weaned child shall put its hand on the adder's den.
> They will not hurt or destroy
>   on all my holy mountain;
> for the earth will be full of the knowledge of the Lord
>   as the waters cover the sea.
>
> Isaiah 11:6–9

Much more recently, in 1850, it was the conflict between belief in a loving creator and the cruelty and suffering in the natural world that led Tennyson to write in *In Memoriam*:

> Man ...
> Who trusted God was love indeed
>   And love Creation's final law —
>   Tho' Nature, red in tooth and claw
> With ravin, shriek'd against his creed ...

How do we respond to this dilemma? Most people who believe in a divine creator of the universe believe — and almost take it for granted — that the creator is also the source of all goodness, but Mary Midgley (1994) points out that this need not be so: it would be possible to imagine a bad creator who created us for bad purposes. Another way out of the dilemma would be to follow the Christian lecturer in Edinburgh in the 1850s who, according to Hugh Miller (1857), told his audience that, though God created all the wild animals, it was the devil who made the flesh-eaters among them fierce and carnivorous. Other people have found that they cannot believe in a divine creator at all. Each of these three philosophical positions regards the moral sense (about the cruelty of the natural world) as authoritative and non-negotiable, but each is willing to give up belief in a good, all-powerful God: the first suggests that God might not be good, the second that God might not be all-powerful, and the third that God might not exist at all.

Christian theologians, in contrast, are more inclined to seek ways to reconcile the two, without compromising their belief in a good and all-powerful God or denying our human sense that he allows cruelty and suffering to exist.

The cruelty of nature offends against our moral sense. As with our sense of fairness, this aspect of our moral thinking runs against the grain of the universe we inhabit.

How We Treat Other Species

Apart from care of the young and, occasionally, the vulnerable (Section 3-1), kindness to other species is a human quality. Other animals generally have no concern for the suffering of other species. The cat with a mouse, the snake with its prey, chimpanzees hunting and killing a colobus monkey or baboon are just a few examples among many. There is no understanding of what it is to make another animal suffer, and no abhorrence of it.

Many humans, before modern times, were able to combine a respect for the souls of other animals with an unquestioning, pragmatic acceptance of the need to kill them for food. Frazer (1922) gives examples from all over the world and points out that 'savages' considered that animals possessed intelligence, feelings and souls, like humans: they did not make a sharp distinction between humans and other animals. For Socrates and Aristotle, however, animals existed for the sake of man (Wise, 2001), and this view has permeated much of subsequent Western thinking.

If we look at the British, who are renowned for their love of animals, we can see a progression over the last two hundred years, by which activities that were once thought morally acceptable come to be seen as cruel and unacceptable. The first legislation against cruelty to animals was in 1822, and the SPCA (later to become the RSPCA) was founded two years later. Bear-baiting and cock-fighting were outlawed in 1835 and 1849 respectively. This progression has continued up to the present time. The public mood in Britain has been to impose ever stricter controls on animal experiments. Vegetarianism is more widespread than it used to be.

Peter Vardy and Paul Grosch (1999) list five controversial issues in the way we treat other animals: animals bred and killed for food; animals used for medical experiments; animals used for the testing of cosmetics, detergents and other non-medical goods; animals bred and killed for their fur; and animals hunted and killed for sport, and bred and trained for entertainment. Steven Wise's ground-breaking and thought-provoking *Rattling the Cage* (2001) argues for legal rights for animals, starting with chimpanzees and bonobos, and Jane Goodall, in a Foreword to the book, points out how much change there had been in public attitudes in the last years of the twentieth century.

It is not easy to explain this propensity for kindness to animals or the growth of this sentiment in recent years in terms of any of the usual perspectives on moral thinking. It is not a sentiment that we share with other primates, so it is not likely to be inherited from our pre-human ancestors. Chimpanzees have no scruple about killing monkeys (fellow primates) for food; the kind of argument put forward by Steven Wise, for example, who pleads for humans to show special concern in the way we treat other primates, our nearest animal relatives, would cut no ice with a chimpanzee.

Christians will find that there is little teaching in the Bible on the subject of kindness or cruelty to animals. Humans are given the responsibility to look after the rest of the natural creation and to care for their animals, but they are also taught that they are the highest order of creation, superior to other animals. Traditionally, the Christian church has not given animal welfare a high priority as a moral issue.

Kindness to animals is not necessarily linked with altruism or goodwill towards other humans. Certainly some more extreme forms of cruelty to animals, where cruelty is the only purpose, may indicate a cruel nature which may also find expression in cruelty to humans, but this does not apply to the sort of issues that are currently under debate. Meat eaters and livestock farmers are no more cruel or uncaring than vegetarians. People who use animals as an aid to medical research are working for the good of other people.

Concern for animal welfare is not linked to a rational principle — biodiversity, for example. Quite the reverse, in fact. The use of animals for human purposes increases or maintains biodiversity, and banning them runs a risk of reducing biodiversity.

Finally, the growth of this concern for animal well-being runs counter to natural selection and evolutionary correctness. Humans are more likely to prosper, as individuals and as a species, if we are willing to countenance the use of animals in medical research and, more generally, if we have an ethic that permits us to use animals for our benefit. If natural selection were the dominant influence on us, our only concern for animal welfare would be to look after the health of those animals that we require for our own use and to ensure that no useful species dies out.

However, if we take the approach set out on page 34, we can make better sense of it. We care about animals because it is in our nature to care — particularly for those who are weaker and more vulnerable than ourselves. It is also in our nature to be able to imagine their suffering and to have sympathy for them. This links in with the moral indignation we feel about cruelty in nature (page 72). Our knowledge and understanding of our own suffering leads us to a concern about suffering in different species.

We have noted the trend towards increasing concern for animal welfare, as we look back from the beginning of the twenty-first century. Charles Darwin made the same observation in *The Descent of Man* 130 years earlier. He, and we, can see this as the culmination of a trend, which started with our obligation and concern for the well-being of our own offspring and family (inherited from our pre-human ancestors). This concern widened to include, first, the tribe, then the nation, then all of humanity, and now other animal species. When *The Descent of Man* was published, concern for animal welfare was less developed than it is today, but Darwin recognised it as an important, and relatively recent, aspect of the moral sense and he regarded it as a natural step in the development of moral thinking:

> Sympathy beyond the confines of man, that is, humanity to the lower animals, seems to be one of the latest moral acquisitions. It is apparently unfelt by savages, except towards their pets. How little the old Romans knew of it is shown by their abhorrent gladiatorial exhibitions. The very idea of humanity, as far as I could observe, was new to most of the Gauchos of the Pampas. This virtue, one of the noblest with which man is endowed, seems to arise incidentally from our sympathies becoming more tender and more widely diffused, until they are extended to all sentient beings. As soon as this virtue is honoured and practised by some few men, it spreads

through instruction and example to the young, and eventually becomes incorporated in public opinion.

The idea of caring concern extending outwards from the family to the tribe to the nation to all of humanity and finally to all sentient beings has been taken up by Peter Singer in *The Expanding Circle*, quoted on page 67.

Preserving the Planet

The technological advances and population growth of recent decades have enabled the human species to influence the physical and biological systems of the earth far more drastically than ever before. In his classic book *Planetary Overload* (1993), A J McMichael reviews six main threats to the future health and well-being of human populations: population increase, poverty and health; greenhouse warming and climate change; the thinning ozone layer; soil and water (agriculture, food and fisheries); biodiversity; and the growth of cities. These threats are relatively new: 'Compared with the hunter-gatherer era, which predominated until a short 10,000 years ago, human numbers have multiplied one thousand fold (including a massive ten-fold increase in the last 250 years) and our average, daily, per-person energy use is also about one thousand times greater' (McMichael, 1993).

We can acknowledge these facts about environmental change and the threats for the future, but the question then arises, 'Should they be regarded as moral issues?' It is one thing to state facts, it is another to incorporate them into our moral thinking: to make the transition from an 'is' to an 'ought' (see page 25). When we are faced with these facts, do they trigger some long-established moral principle? It is only recently that we have come to recognise how serious the issues are, so they are not considered directly in traditional moral teaching and thinking. They are not taken as seriously as some of our long-established moral principles, like those against lying and stealing — but perhaps the future well-being of the human species will depend on us taking them more seriously.

When we consider these threats to the future of the human species, we are looking at the long-term consequences of the way we treat our environment, and the moral argument will therefore be a consequentialist argument — based, perhaps, on the principles of family first and caring concern for all. McMichael (1993) writes of the 'general moral problem ... of bequeathing to future generations a negative legacy, an ecologically damaged world.' The damage results from individual choices about our lifestyle and level of consumption. We may like to think that the issues are matters for the government to deal with (and governments can do a great deal in promoting energy-saving technologies, for example, and encouraging us to reduce our consumption) but in a free country the power of government to influence our lifestyle and our personal consumption is very limited. The real power lies with us as individuals: decisions made by millions of people, cumulatively, can make a huge difference. We can make a huge difference — and yet the decisions made by one person alone make no difference at all in the long term. This is where, as a moral issue, acting for the good of the planet differs from most day-to-day moral issues. We can see the value of every little deed of kindness or honesty, for example, regardless of how other people are behaving. It is more difficult to see the long-term benefit of the small reductions that we can make to our consumption, when we can see other people increasing theirs without a thought.

We may be more likely to take environmental issues seriously if we can relate them to moral principles that have a greater immediacy. Extravagance and waste have long been regarded as moral issues ('Waste not, want not'; 'Make do and mend'). Wanton destruction has also been regarded as a moral issue. Mary Midgley (1983) illustrates this in an article entitled 'Duties concerning Islands', in which she asks her readers to imagine that, before leaving his island, Robinson Crusoe had decided to set fire to it and devastate it. It is clearly her intention that her readers should feel a moral abhorrence at such senseless destruction. Considerations like these can encourage us to think in moral terms about our own lifestyles and also about the kind of government policies that we would support. The world-wide pattern of increasing consumption of energy and other resources suggests that, whatever the rhetoric, most people are more concerned with increasing their living standards than they are with protecting the environment.

Thoughts

Charles Darwin had a clear view of progress in moral thinking. As we have seen, he regarded kindness to animals as an expression of an advanced morality. The passage on kindness to animals quoted on page 75 is followed immediately by the following:

> The highest possible stage in moral culture is when we recognise that we ought to control our thoughts, and 'not even in inmost thought to think again the sins that made the past so pleasant to us.' [Tennyson] Whatever makes any bad action familiar to the mind, renders its performance by so much the easier. As Marcus Aurelius

long ago said, 'Such as are thy habitual thoughts, such also will be
the character of thy mind; for the soul is dyed by the thoughts.'

This vision of a future when sin and temptation are no more accords
with Dante's (1320: Canto IX) vision of paradise:

> But here there's no repentance; here we smile —
>   Not at the sin, which comes no more to mind,
>   but at God's ordering touch, His master-style.

C S Lewis (1964) agrees: 'There is no morality in Heaven. ... the
blessed dead have long since gladly forgotten it.'

A noble vision, this. Were we to achieve Darwin's ideal, we
would never experience bad thoughts and never experience temptation — and that would be an end to human nature as we know it.
The human mind is inherently undisciplined. It lets us down in so
many ways. We may think it makes us wise, but we're only part way
to wisdom: *Homo semi-sapiens*. Konrad Lorenz (1966) suggested that
'the long-sought missing link between animals and the really
humane being is ourselves' and expressed the hope that 'from us
human beings something better and higher may evolve.' Perhaps
one day our descendents will deserve to be known as *Homo sapiens*.

The passage from Darwin and his quotation from Marcus
Aurelius lead us naturally to the question of character and personal
integrity.

Personal Integrity

Most writers on moral issues concentrate on the social aspects: love,
compassion, altruism, honesty and, generally, behaviour that does
good to other people and brings them happiness. These are, perhaps, the most important aspects of the moral sense, but they are not
the whole picture. Part of moral thinking relates to our own personal integrity, and has little to do with anyone else. 'Human beings
extend the scope of their moral rules into areas of "private" life
where the social consequences of behaviour, whether good or bad,
are to say the least unclear' (Wright, 1971). Bertrand Russell (1954)
also points out that ethics cannot be wholly social. This aspect of
moral thinking is represented in the writings of Aristotle and,
recently, in the concept of virtue ethics (e.g. Darwall, 2003). Virtue
ethics is concerned primarily with character rather than conduct.

Integrity has to do with one's own self-image, often related to the
notion of self-discipline and self-denial. Some of our achievements
are purely personal. They are of no interest or concern to anyone
else; perhaps nobody else even knows about them (our personal
achievements at activities like jogging or crossword puzzles, for

example). We set the rules, and we keep them — or we cheat. It is not altruism that stops us cheating: it is our own personal integrity.

We may have opportunities to steal, to take a hypothetical situation we have used before: we won't get caught, no one will know, and the company, with its multi-million pound turnover, won't be hurt by the loss of £100. What prevents us? It is our own sense of honesty, of integrity, of the kind of people we consider ourselves to be. We could extend this illustration and say that the stolen £100 would save a life or relieve suffering. Altruism might argue for theft (the Robin Hood scenario), but we would be restrained by our conscience.

Personal integrity is under threat today. A moral code that puts all the emphasis on doing good to others will not have much room for personal integrity, and nor will a consequentialist code (Williams, 1973). It is possible to present arguments in favour of social morality without appealing to moral thinking at all, just asking people to think about the consequences of bad behaviour: being found out, punishment, people thinking badly of you, losing friends, and so on. It is more difficult to make a case for personal integrity, however, to people who don't see the point of moral behaviour or moral thinking as ends in themselves. And yet we could argue that personal integrity — our sense of the kind of person we want to be — is the basis for all of our moral thinking and behaviour, underpinning everything else.

Chapter 4

Towards a New Consensus

4-1. Trying to Account for the Moral Mind

All science is preliminary and we have to recognise and make the best of our ignorance.

Gabriel Dover, *Dear Mr Darwin*

The more we look at the moral mind, the more we can assert with confidence that the moral sense is a significant and important part of the human personality and that it expresses more than just a personal opinion. When we use the words 'good, 'bad' and 'ought', they mean something, although the full meanings of these words may be beyond our grasp or comprehension. We recognise that there is a subjective element in our moral judgements, but we also know that in making our subjective judgements we are struggling to express real, objective values. Our own values are a reflection — but an imperfect reflection — of these objective values.

There have been many attempts to understand and explain the moral sense and moral values. They have one outstanding characteristic in common: they all fail. The great philosophers have, of course, made huge contributions to human understanding, but not one of them has produced a theory of ethics that comes near to being universally accepted. Authoritative books on ethics (e.g. Singer, 1994) summarise the ideas of several different philosophers and schools of philosophy, and each such summary is followed by the arguments against: explanations as why the ideas fail. Some are criticised on rational grounds, but others fail because in some situations they lead to conclusions that are contrary to widely held moral convictions. The latter is the ultimate test: any theory will fail if it conflicts with our moral convictions.

Two conclusions follow from this. The first is that it is very remarkable that such an important part of the human personality remains so little understood that several widely differing, and contrasting, theories are still promulgated, even though there is wide agreement that each is defective. The second is that if moral convictions have been able to undermine every theory that has been proposed — it just shows how powerful the moral sense is, able to triumph over every theory that we can put forward in our attempts to pin it down and constrain it. For the moral sense cannot be defined in terms of anything else. It cuts across all other aspects of the human personality. It cuts across our emotional desires and our likes and dislikes. It cuts across our sense of scientific rationality. It cuts across our instinctive patterns of behaviour, inherited from our pre-human primate ancestors. It cuts across our wish to behave like the people around us. It cuts across our observations of the natural world. It even cuts across the Christian understanding of God. Our moral autonomy is independent of all of these — potentially a very powerful force.

Part of the value of carrying out a survey like that in Chapter 3 is that it provides a body of evidence against which to test any theory or explanation of morality. We have noted some examples as we went along; we shall now see what conclusions we can draw.

Several writers have suggested that an evolutionary understanding of the origin of the moral sense makes it unnecessary to believe in God. This oversimplifies the possible roles of God and of evolution, and we shall look at these issues later in the chapter. But first we shall examine the suggestion that the moral sense is inevitable in human-like beings and that its existence can be understood in terms of natural selection.

Is the Moral Sense Inevitable?

Charles Darwin (1874) considered that 'any animal whatever, endowed with well-marked social instincts, the parental and filial affections being here included, would inevitably acquire a moral sense or conscience, as soon as its intellectual powers had become as well, or nearly as well, developed as in man.' His argument is based, in part, on the ability of humans to reflect on past behaviour. This can lead to regret, remorse or repentance: 'A moral being is one who is capable of comparing his past and future actions, or motives, and of approving or disapproving of them.' We have a conscience. We are also aware of the approval or disapproval of others.

The main points in Darwin's hypothesis (inevitability, social instincts, intellectual powers, reflection on the past) have been taken up by several recent writers. Sociobiologists, for example, would attribute the moral sense directly to natural selection: 'Morality, or more particularly the moral sense, comes about because the moral human has more chance of surviving and reproducing than the immoral person' (Ruse, 1979). Peter Singer (1994) writes that 'we can understand ethics as a natural phenomenon that arises in the course of the evolution of social, intelligent long-lived mammals who possess the capacity to recognise each other and to remember the past behaviour of others.' Frans de Waal (2001, quoted at greater length on page 59) also places the moral sense in an evolutionary context: 'Instead of seeing morality as a radically new invention, I tend to view it as a natural outgrowth of ancient social tendencies.'

Is this thesis persuasive? Is it 'inevitable' that a being with the intellectual and social attributes of humans would acquire a moral sense? To put it another way, could a human-like creature exist without a moral sense? I shall endeavour to show that the inevitability argument does not stand up to scrutiny — but I should like to make it clear that in doing so I am not implying that the moral sense could not have arisen by the natural processes of evolution: clearly, the moral sense has developed in humans. Where I take issue with the hypotheses put forward by Darwin and the sociobiologists is in their belief that the development of the moral sense was 'inevitable', and in the implication that it can be understood in terms of natural selection. Rather, I agree with Railton (2000): 'Neither human morality nor human scientific practice is comfortably described as "the product of natural selection"'.

There are five points to make here. The first is to say again that behaving well is not the same as having a moral sense. The second is that a look around the animal kingdom shows that conscience is not the best way to promote good behaviour: instincts are more effective. The third is that, in practice, natural selection does not necessarily favour moral behaviour. The fourth is that the ability to reflect on the past only leads to moral behaviour if we are that way inclined anyway. Fifthly and finally, we shall examine the implied belief that an intelligent, social, human-like species could not exist and prosper without a moral sense.

The *first point*, that behaving well is not the same as having a moral sense, is basic to an understanding of the moral sense (page 5). The conceptual distinction between behavioural tendencies and moral judgement was noted more than a century ago by Thomas Henry Huxley (1895): 'Cosmic evolution may teach us how the good and the evil tendencies of man may have come about; but, in itself, it is incompetent to furnish any better reason why what we call good is preferable to what we call evil than we had before.' The importance of distinguishing between behaviour and the moral sense is also emphasised by Kummer (2000), Railton (2000) and Troyer (2000) in their discussion of Flack and de Waal (2000).

To turn to the *second objection*, we can see that this 'good' behaviour in other animals is effectively enforced by instinct (see Section 3-1). The social insects, for example, work tirelessly for the common good. They have no understanding of the Protestant work ethic, but their instinctive dedication to the common good surpasses that of any human. There are two senses in which we might describe such behaviour as 'good': it is successful in terms of survival, and it is approved of by our human moral sense. The insects have no moral understanding, but their instinct is a more effective influence than any human conscience.[1]

Then, some human societies consider that mating for life is morally good. This is a lifestyle which is followed by several other animal species: jackdaws, bullfinches, greylag geese and other birds, for example, and our closer relatives the gibbons. These animals are not motivated by moral sentiments. They are following their instincts, and these instincts control their behaviour more effectively than the human moral sense. In many human societies, incest and adultery are both regarded as morally wrong. As we have seen, the former is inhibited by instincts inherited from our pre-human ancestors, supported by moral sanction; the latter by moral sanction alone. It is notable that the inhibition against incest is generally more effective than that against adultery.

Konrad Lorenz (1952) illustrated his own faith in the power of instinct — compared with his rather weaker confidence in human moral restraint — with a story about onlookers who reproached him for allowing a raven to groom him, with raven beak close to human eye. Lorenz replied that he felt in less danger from the bird than from the onlooker: the instinctive restraint of the former was more reliable than the moral restraint of the latter, should he for some unaccountable reason wish to shoot his host.

My argument is that instinct, honed by natural selection, is a more effective force for good behaviour than any amount of moral philosophy or preaching or conscience. If a certain type of behaviour is a real help for survival, that behaviour will be more securely established in the lifestyle of the species if it is instinctive than if individu-

---

[1] Go to the ant, Immanuel Kant;
     Consider her ways and be wise.
     She works like a beauty — with no sense of duty
     And no need to philosophise!

als possess a moral sense combined with the freedom to make their own choices. The existence of a moral sense implies freedom, temptation and lapses from the 'good'. It is not an effective way of enforcing 'good' behaviour.

It can be argued that once you have creatures with free will and the ability to make choices to the extent that humans can, some sort of moral conscience is essential to control our wayward behaviour. Does this invalidate my argument? Mary Midgley (1994), for example, argues that the removal of instinctive constraints gives us freedom, and it is this freedom that makes moral constraints necessary. Has instinct lost the power to control our behaviour, leaving a vacuum that must be filled? Looking at humans, I don't think that this is the case. Even in humans, instinct is more effective than moral dictates, and even in humans, instinct is still there to exert its influence on our free will where it really matters. This is natural selection in action. Let me explain.

If natural selection were to write a list of commandments, what would come top of the list? What are the essential elements of behaviour if a human being (or any other animal) is to survive and have descendents? I think there are four that are more important than any others: (1) feed; (2) remain alive for long enough to have children; (3) have children; and (4) make sure that the children are cared for until they can look after themselves. For most humans, these commandments are adequately enforced by instinct. Robert Hinde (2002) observes that looking after our children is such a natural thing to do that we seldom think of it as a moral precept. In all these four elements of behaviour, we have free will and we exercise free will; but the choices we make are influenced more by instinct than by moral considerations. The existence of a conscious, intelligent intellect does not, it seems, inevitably lead to the breakdown of instinctive constraints. Much human behaviour, in addition to these four important elements, is ruled, or strongly influenced, by powerful instincts.

Let us try, for a moment, to imagine what it would be like if our four commandments of natural selection were under the control of the moral sense, not instinct, so that most of us had no natural inclination to feed, no inclination to stay alive, no inclination to have children, and no inclination to care for children; and if we only did these things reluctantly, because our consciences told us to. With the rather weak consciences that most of us have, I doubt that the human species would have lasted long, but if it did, and if a strong conscience was inheritable, there is no doubt that we would have found that, over time, natural selection would have favoured those with strong consciences — which leads to my third point.

The *third objection* is that natural selection does not necessarily favour the kind of behaviour that the moral sense approves of. Human behaviour is not conspicuously 'better' than that of other, morality-free animals (Lorenz, 1966; Flack and de Waal, 2000). Huxley (1895) pointed out that immoral sentiments and behaviour in humans are as much the product of evolution as moral sentiments and behaviour, and of course this is true of other animals as well. It is often observed that immoral behaviour in humans prospers just as well as moral behaviour. Some 3000 years ago, the psalmist wrote 'I saw the prosperity of the wicked. ... Such are the wicked; always at ease, they increase in riches' (Psalm 73), and today it is just as easy to make a case for a decline in moral standards and the ever-increasing success of unprincipled people as it is to make a case for the opposite.

If we look at the evidence presented in this book, what light does it throw? I think that we can see that where the moral sense is aligned with the natural-selection-honed instincts that we have inherited from our pre-human primate ancestors, it is very largely superfluous ('If parents invariably love their children, what would be the point of having a moral principle that tells parents that they ought to love their children?'; Sober and Wilson, 2000); where it is opposed to these instincts, it is not determined by natural selection.

Neither natural selection nor conscience have made us behave particularly morally, then. Insofar as we do follow our consciences, we can be led to some behaviour that favours the survival of our genes (looking after our children, for example), but there are other moral convictions that 'do not favour but even hinder the survival and reproduction of individuals and their genes' (Stenmark, 2001). A particularly good example of the latter, as we have noted, is our concern for animal welfare. 'Ethical systems — even in the rare cases where they are acted upon by a majority of the population for most of the time — cannot be regarded as necessarily conferring a selective breeding advantage on their practitioners' (de Reuck, 1969).

Fourthly, what about Darwin's point that humans can reflect on their actions and experience regret, repentance and remorse? The ability to reflect on the past is an essential part of what it is to be human — but it has no moral implications. This ability can lead to regret, but again there are no moral implications: it is true that a bungled burglary can lead the would-be thieves to repent of their life of crime (a moral reaction), but it can equally lead them to regret the failure of their latest enterprise, learn from their mistakes, and go on to achieve a more polished performance next time — and this is nothing to do with morality.

How would our capacity to reflect and regret affect us if our motives were guided not by moral thinking but by instincts which, in turn, were controlled by natural selection? If we understood the principles of natural selection, we would know that if we behaved in obedience to our natural-selection-honed instincts we and our children would prosper: if we acted against them, we would not. We would behave accordingly. Our thinking would be purely pragmatic. There would be no need for a moral dimension.

This leads to my *fifth point* for consideration: would it be possible for an intelligent, social being to exist and prosper without a moral sense at all? Darwin and others imply that natural selection would select against such a creature: in the preceding paragraphs I have argued against this thesis. Colin McGinn (1979) recognises that moral principle is contrary to natural selection, and tries to explain its existence by suggesting that morality is a by-product of an evolutionarily useful intelligence (in rather the same way as sickle-cell anaemia is a by-product of protection against malaria: page 33) — but he offers no evidence or argument in support of this idea.

From a theoretical point of view, it is quite possible to imagine a human-like being with the sort of instincts that natural selection would favour but with no moral sense. The drivers for behavioural choices would be these instincts (as we have seen with the four most important behavioural elements), plus the range of human emotions. Emotions and instincts that were seriously harmful would not be selected. Conscious thought would be used in a pragmatic way to work out how to achieve the objectives set by these instincts and emotions: to find the best food, secure the best mate, decide how many children to have, provide the best upbringing for the children, avoid conflict wherever possible so as to enable the family to survive, and look after the environment for future generations. You have only to read this list to realise that natural selection, instinct and pragmatic, conscious decision-making could provide the basis for a more evolutionarily successful existence than that created by our supposedly 'moral', but thoughtless, temptation-prone and wilful, species — *Homo semi-sapiens*.

For much of the time most humans do actually follow instinct, emotion and pragmatic thinking, with no moral considerations. Our moral sense can give meaning and purpose to life, but we can (and often do) derive our sense of purpose from elsewhere (money, power, achievement, relationships with other people, for example). The morality-free model of the human personality presented by psychologists (page 19) is seriously flawed, but it is plausible. Humans are not like that — but we could have been.

Moral behaviour does not correlate with possession of a conscience (various writers from Aristotle onwards have suggested that it correlates more with strength of will). Prisons are not full of people devoid of conscience. Many prisoners are rounded men and women, possessing a moral sense — but people who are still capable of doing dreadful things (in the words of a prison chaplain, Robert Davies (1993), 'Words ... such as love, forgiveness and reconciliation ... come alive for many people in prison.'). Conversely, there are people with only a weak moral sense or none at all (the amoral character) who find that there are sound, pragmatic reasons of self-interest for following the moral code of those about them (Wright, 1971).[2]

For examples of what human nature could be like we can look to the world of fiction. A novel gives an imaginative writer an opportunity to try out an idea about human nature and see if it works. Let us compare three very different novels, all of them plausible and convincing portrayals of human nature, Jane Austen's *Emma*, P G Wodehouse's *Summer Lightning* and Alexander McCall Smith's *The Sunday Philosophy Club*. Emma Woodhouse, Lord Emsworth and Isabel Dalhousie are all intelligent people, often motivated by personal ambition and self-interest, who, by and large, like to live in peace and harmony with those around them; but they differ in the part that moral thinking plays in their lives.

Isabel Dalhousie in *The Sunday Philosophy Club* spends much of her time pondering on moral issues — and is aware that she doesn't always live up to her moral principles. The exploration of ethical issues and her own moral sense are important to her, and she recognises the moral dimension in many of the little happenings and decisions of daily life.

Jane Austen's Emma Woodhouse also recognises the importance of the moral dimension (and when she forgets, her lapse is drawn to her attention by Mr Knightley), but for the most part daily life is conducted without recourse to moral thinking.

---

[2] These self-controlled amoral people, who work out that 'moral' behaviour may be in their own best interests, are not psychopaths. The psychopathic personality is a personality disorder with characteristics that include an inability to tolerate minor frustrations, an incapacity for forming stable relationships, a failure to learn from experience and a tendency to act recklessly (Gregory, 2004).

Lord Emsworth and P G Wodehouse's other characters, in contrast, are happily ignorant of what the moral dimension is all about. They inhabit a world described by Stephen Fry as 'prelapsarian' and by Robert McCrum (2004) as Wodehouse's 'own lunatic Eden'. Disagreeable emotions like 'conscience' and 'guilt' do intrude on rare occasions, but they are mercifully short-lived and are not expected to have any significant influence over the way anyone behaves. For the most part, human behaviour is described in a non-judgemental way and the thought processes by which the characters are led to their decisions are inspired by simple desires and emotions (love, acquisitiveness, ambition, pleasure, loyalty to friends etc), free of any moral considerations or restraints. The thought processes themselves are far from simple, involving detailed consideration of the existing situation and the possible consequences of proposed courses of action as the characters work their way through the tortuous ramifications of a Wodehouse plot. Like the pre-human, animal world, this amoral, prelapsarian Eden includes deeds that we would call 'morally bad' – deceit and theft, for example — and they take their place as part of the pattern of life. Wodehouse's stories show how easy it is to imagine intelligent, social humans, or human-like creatures, driven by instinct, emotion, self-interest and intelligent, pragmatic reasoning — without any real awareness of the moral dimension.[3]

We can therefore conclude that the logic of natural selection would not lead to a moral (or part-moral) species like humans as we know them. Natural selection is not sufficient to account for the moral sense.

Summing Up

It is sometimes suggested that an evolutionary understanding of morality makes it unnecessary to believe in God. This implies that

---

[3]   As the books, so the man. Reading about his life you get the impression of a man who didn't make moral judgements and seemed to be rather perplexed when other people made moral judgements about him. His broadcasts from Berlin during the war, following his release from the rigours and hardships of a German prison camp for civil internees, were in his usual style, only perhaps rather more zany ('Young men starting off in life have often asked me, "How can I become an internee?" …'). His failure to make moral judgements about his captors — and, indeed, his willingness to make the broadcasts at all — was not well received in wartime England. As Malcolm Muggeridge wrote, 'He is a man singularly ill-fitted to live in a time of ideological conflict, having no feelings of hatred about anyone and no very strong views about anything. In the behaviour of his fellow humans, whoever they may be, he detects nothing more pernicious than a kind of sublime idiocy …' (Connolly, 1979).

evolution and divine creation are mutually exclusive, and that the role of religion is to provide us with an explanation of something for which we do not have a scientific explanation (an approach known as 'the god of the gaps'). Both of these implications should be challenged. Science and religion should not be regarded as irreconcilable alternatives: both are concerned with our attempts to understand the universe we live in, and in this fundamental sense they are partners in the same great enterprise. If science *does* have a satisfactory explanation for something, we cannot rule out the possibility that there was some guidance from the creator, acting through the (divinely created) laws of nature. Equally, if science *does not* have a satisfactory explanation for something, we cannot rule out the possibility that it may come up with a good explanation in the future. Neither the theologian nor the scientist has to be able to have an answer for everything. It should be quite possible for both to be able to say of the moral sense, for example, 'I don't know. We can attempt to describe it but we can't explain it.'

Those who believe in a divine creator cannot expect that an understanding of every aspect of creation should be within their grasp.[4] It is possible that the belief by some Christians that the human mind is capable of understanding and explaining everything about the divine creator is, at least in part, responsible for the fact that religion has been on the retreat intellectually during the scientific age, as one dogma after another, supposedly part of the Christian religion but in fact a human construct, has been found to conflict with scientific understanding.

Similarly, those who look to science to make sense of the world will know that the history of science is full of situations in which existing theory has been unable to account for observed phenomena: sometimes, with the passage of time, new evidence or new insights help us to advance our understanding. Scientists, too, have been known to make exaggerated claims for the achievements of science.

We have seen that current scientific understanding, based on the theory of natural selection, does not help us to explain how or why human beings have a sense of moral values. This lack of a scientific explanation could lead to the conclusion that our moral perception comes from God, by direct divine intervention. This 'god of the

[4]   E.g. 'Can you find out the deep things of God? Can you find out the limit of the Almighty?' (Job 11:7); 'Such knowledge is too wonderful for me; it is so high that I cannot attain it (Psalm 139:6); '[The creator's] understanding is unsearchable' (Isaiah 40:28); 'For now we see in a mirror, dimly' (1 Corinthians 13:12).

gaps' type of theory would have to be revised if and when science offered a plausible explanation. An alternative line of reasoning would be to look at the weakness and inadequacy of the moral sense in general and guilt in particular, which, as we have seen, are (surprisingly and puzzlingly) ineffective at guiding and controlling our behaviour; to observe those aspects (our sense of fairness and our abhorrence of cruelty in nature) that are contrary to the grain of the universe; and to conclude from this general impression of disarray that direct divine intervention may be a less likely explanation than an origin through some natural biological process that we do not yet understand ('Anything produced by evolution is bound to be a mess'; Dover, 2000a).[5]

In Chapter 1, I distinguished four separate issues, all of them included in the overall concept of morality, and emphasised the need to be clear about them when considering origins or explanations. We can summarise how far we have got in our attempt to understand their origins as follows:

Objective morality: absolute moral values, of which our own, subjective, moral sense offers an imperfect reflection, as we strive for greater understanding. I have argued that our subjective moral feelings only make sense if objective values exist. As a Christian myself, I see God as creator of the universe and its natural scientific laws, and also as the author and authority of absolute moral values — though I am left puzzled that these objective values are not clearer to us. Other writers see objective values as inherent in the human mind or brain. Simon Blackburn (2001), for example, writes of 'small, unpretentious things that we know with perfect certainty', like 'happiness is preferable to misery, and dignity is better than humiliation', and Michael Gazzaniga (2005) supports 'the idea that there could be a universal set of biological responses to moral dilemmas, a sort of ethics, built into our brains.' For all of us, though, there is a great deal about objective morality that remains a mystery.

The moral sense: the mental attribute that leads us to seek to understand moral values and apply them in our lives, and enables us to recognise and resist temptation and to pass moral judgement on our own behaviour and that of other people. We have seen that it is rea-

---

[5]   It is interesting to note that, in the Genesis story, it was not in God's plan that humans should have the knowledge of good and evil: it was not part of the original creation (Genesis 1–2). Adam and Eve gained this knowledge as a consequence — one might say a 'natural', unavoidable, consequence — of their disobedience (Genesis 3). Before that, in the prelapsarian world of the Garden of Eden, the earliest humans lived without a knowledge of good and evil — without a moral sense.

sonable to postulate an origin involving natural processes, though not driven by natural selection. The moral sense is firmly rooted in the human mind and engages with various aspects of the human personality to give each human being their own unique blend of moral values. It is reasonable to suggest that the moral sense itself is hard-wired, but there is a certain amount of diversity between individuals in the way it is expressed. Although the existence of the moral sense itself is hard to account for, we have seen that it is possible to understand some of its manifestations in the context of our animal ancestry and some others by looking at the importance humans attach to conformity to custom.

Behaviour that we may choose to class as good or bad. We have seen that an understanding of our animal ancestry can help us to make sense of a great deal of our behaviour and the thinking that lies behind it — but not all of it. Specifically, we saw (page 34) how our human capacity for showing caring concern for all may have evolved from the earliest examples of parental care.

Moral codes. These derive from the moral sense, and represent our attempts to reflect objective moral values and see how they can be applied at a practical level.

4-2. Some Conclusions

Know then thyself, presume not God to scan,
The proper study of mankind is man.
Placed on this isthmus of a middle state,
A being darkly wise, and rudely great:
With too much knowledge for the sceptic side,
With too much weakness for the stoic's pride,
He hangs between; in doubt to act or rest;
In doubt to deem himself a god, or beast;
In doubt his mind or body to prefer;
Born but to die, and reasoning but to err;
Alike in ignorance, his reason such,
Whether he thinks too little or too much;
Chaos of Thought and Passion, all confused;
Still by himself abused or disabused;
Created half to rise, and half to fall;
Great lord of all things, yet a prey to all;
Sole judge of truth, in endless error hurl'd:
The glory, jest and riddle of the world!

Alexander Pope, *An Essay on Man*

These words of Alexander Pope capture the paradox of human nature, the paradox of *Homo semi-sapiens*. Pre-human creatures had no knowledge of right and wrong. They did as they did, they fought and they strived, they suffered and they died, and that was that.

This is what we see in non-human animals today. And then a new kind of being emerged, 'placed on this isthmus of a middle state'. We have 'intimations of a level of reality beyond the narrowly material or the purely biological' (O'Hear, 1999). Much of our behaviour is like that of other animals, but we have a sense of the transcendent, thoughts of immortality, a belief that there are right ways and wrong ways to behave, and aspirations to understand and make sense of it all. As for the future, beyond the isthmus, it is possible to imagine, with Dante and Darwin, that morality will no longer be an issue.

In this perspective, morality is something transient: part of our present 'middle state', but not belonging to the past or future. We have also seen that from the perspective of natural selection morality is of little importance: what matters is to survive, to breed, and to ensure that our offspring survive and breed. If we take the long view, then, morality may seem to be no more than a curious anomaly, but if we take the short view, if we narrow our focus to look at the present, at human beings as we are, morality is supremely important. The moral mind is a tremendously important part of what it is to be human. Moral thinking must have a significant place in our lives if we are to be true to our human nature and live satisfying and fulfilled lives.[6]

We have been looking particularly at how evolution and our animal ancestry might help in the understanding of the moral mind, and have concluded that although evolutionary theory does little to help us understand the existence of the moral sense our animal inheritance does help us to understand some of the moral sentiments that we find within us. I have suggested that when humans acquired a moral sense, it engaged with the complex mixture of instincts, emotions and intellect that make up our human nature:

- It reinforced our inherited instincts for caring for our own young and for other young and needy individuals, as well as our instincts for cooperation, retaliation, conflict avoidance, incest avoidance, warfare, and respect for life, property and truth.

- It combined with our inherited sense of envy and our new-found ability to imagine another's predicament to give us a deep-rooted sense of fairness.

---

[6]   We may from time to time be drawn to the contrary view, of course — that morality interferes with our wish to lead satisfying and fulfilled lives — but this is to take a rather narrow view of morality.

- It combined with our inherited fear of punishment from authority to make us prone to feelings of guilt.

- It reinforced our herd instinct, the tendency to conform to the customs of our own people, and it then got diverted into supporting a great variety of specific customs. It also engaged with our newly acquired independence of mind, enabling us to question the morality of these customs.

- It engaged with our new-found ability to apply our minds beyond the here-and-now, so that our animal instinct for caring and nurturing, guided by empathy and imagination, could be extended, ultimately, to all humans and, further, to other animals.

- It combined with our ability to think about ourselves (our self-consciousness) to develop our sense of personal integrity, the wish to be a moral person and to behave in a moral way even when it affects no one but ourselves.

The modern world has seen the development of new situations, and we have looked at two them: the need to cooperate, economically and in other ways, in very large communities, national and international in scale (page 45), and the need to safeguard the planet as a place fit for human living in centuries to come (page 76). We have seen that our inherited instincts, adapted to the life our ancestors lived many years ago, are inadequate to cope with these situations, and we need a well-developed moral sense, at the level of personal behaviour as well as political principle.

The Moral Dilemma

We must ask moral questions, and we must listen to the answers we receive from our moral sense, our conscience. That is what it means to be human, to be a moral being. And yet we cannot be sure that what our conscience tells us can be relied upon: we must question the answers. We must ask the questions, but we cannot be sure that we can trust the answers: that is the moral dilemma.

If we cannot trust the answers, is there any point in trying to lead a moral life? If there is so much disagreement about moral principles, can we actually be sure of anything? Indeed we can. We cannot stop being moral beings. We have a moral responsibility for how we live our lives, and we cannot escape this responsibility. We have no option but to recognise and accept what it is that makes us human.

Disagreements about moral issues are interesting and there are plenty of them, but there are also very many instances where there is no disagreement. For example, although honesty may sometimes come into conflict with loyalty or kindness (or some other moral principle), most often it does not, and honesty is a clear moral principle to be followed. The same can be said of kindness and other simple moral principles. Consequentialist thinking, too, is often straightforward, leading to an uncontroversial conclusion.

Moral Authority

Until recently it was often believed that religion was the only authority for moral teaching. Today, the authority of religion is very important for some people, but there are many others for whom religion carries little or no authority. It is therefore important for us to seek an approach to moral thinking that does not depend upon the authority of religion.

The three kinds of moral thinking that we have looked at derive their authority from different sources: the first from our instincts; the second from the society we belong to; and the third from beyond these. The moral authority of custom (which often claims, rightly or wrongly, to be backed by religion) can be very strong, and it was not uncommon for twentieth-century writers — as, indeed, Nietzsche before them — to maintain that morality was all a matter of culture. There has been a marked change, though, in recent years in Britain. We have been through a period when all authority was questioned, and the authority of the morality of custom is particularly vulnerable to the relativity argument. It is difficult to claim universal moral authority for a custom when everyone can see that other people are living by different customs, which they consider to be supported by moral thinking. This has led, as we have seen, to the questioning of moral values generally.

The morality of custom is thus being reassessed. A realistic way forward might be for us to recognise the value of conformity as a moral principle, at the same time as acknowledging that many of the customs themselves carry no moral authority. For more secure moral authority we should look to the other two sources, the morality of instinct and the morality of beyond. The behaviour that we endorse may not always be very different, but it will rest on more stable moral foundations. For example, we may continue to regard an ethos of honest trading, fair dealing and public service as morally good. We may no longer be able to promote this by the moral sanction of social convention, but we can re-establish it on the more secure foundations of the morality of instinct (respect for the truth) and the morality of beyond (caring concern for all).

Similarly, we may continue to regard stable family structures and strong family loyalties as good, but the argument will depend less on the moral pressures of social convention (which are breaking down anyway) and more on the morality of instinct (family first, particularly the care of the young) and the morality of beyond (caring concern for all), supported by consequentialist arguments such as the huge social and economic benefits, both to families and to society — arguments powerfully presented with a wealth of supporting evidence by Patricia Morgan (2000, 2004).

Towards a New Morality of Consensus

What many people are looking for today is a new consensus on moral issues. A morality of consensus would resemble the morality of custom in that the strength of its moral principles and moral code would lie in the existence of broad agreement within the community, but whereas the morality of custom tends to be authoritarian, regarding challenge as threatening, the morality of consensus would emerge from vigorous debate in a common cause, a shared exercise in exploration. More important, the morality of custom gives rise to conflict and division, whereas the morality of consensus seeks understanding and, if possible, agreement. As we have seen throughout this book, the morality of instinct and the morality of beyond offer a great deal of common ground between people who are willing to enter into constructive debate, quite enough for us to work towards agreement between people of different traditions, or, where agreement cannot be reached, understanding and acceptance.

If we are to attain a morality of consensus, it is essential that we should recognise both the subjective nature of our own moral sense and the reality of objective morality. Our moral convictions, however strongly held, are our own and we should be willing to challenge them. However, they are pointers towards objective moral values, and it is this search for objective values that unites us all. If we over-emphasise objective morality we forget the frailty and subjective nature of our own moral sentiments; we will take our own moral feelings too seriously and fail to give due consideration to other views. If we over-emphasise subjective morality to the extent of denying the existence of objective values, the search for consensus becomes pointless because all moral values are equally arbitrary; it is a belief in objective values that gives us a shared purpose and makes consensus possible.

Some people may feel that religion is an obstacle in the search for consensus. Some religious people, for example, may think that they have a monopoly of moral principle. If believers use terms like 'the sanctity of human life' and 'the sanctity of marriage', they invite non-believers to take up an opposing point of view — whereas if the same sentiments are expressed in different language ('the value of...' or 'the intrinsic worth of...') there is room for constructive debate. Then again, some non-believers would like to suggest that our moral sentiments have been fed to us down the ages by religious teachers and in a secular society we can and should free ourselves from their constraining influence. Some non-religious people may think that in casting off religion they can cast off most of morality as well. I hope it is clear from this book that the moral mind is not something dreamed up by theologians and religious teachers but is deeply embedded in human nature.

On page 29 I suggested that there was no need for believers and non-believers to disagree on moral issues, and the evidence presented in Chapter 3 provides a great deal of support for this view. The moral sense is deep-rooted and common to all of humanity, and most of our moral sentiments occur independently of religious sentiments. Indeed, they sometimes come into conflict with religious belief and teaching, and when they do we often find that the moral sentiments are the stronger of the two (as we have seen in fairness, for example, and the appearance of cruelty in the natural world). Michael Gazzaniga (2005) comes to a similar conclusion but from a different starting point, that of a neuroscientist: 'It appears that all of us share the same moral networks and systems, and we all respond in similar ways to similar issues.' Where we differ, he suggests, is not so much in our moral responses as in our theoretical understanding of these responses. A rather similar point is made by the Christian theologian Helen Oppenheimer (1965), who wrote that the difference between the believer and the non-believer is 'a difference about the nature of the world, not about the nature of morality.'

Many serious moral issues are complicated, with different points of view that are defensible. Let us take, for example, the issues of abortion, assistance for seriously ill patients who wish to have their lives brought to an early end, arranged marriages, family cohesion and stability, the balance between caring for one's own family and devoting resources of time, energy and money to the wider community and other people and causes, the balance between protection of property and redistribution of income and wealth, the maintenance of different roles for men and women, the balance between caring about animal welfare and using animals to serve human needs, and the balance between consuming the earth's resources for today's needs and conserving them for the future. These are all matters of personal and social morality and they are all controversial, but in most of them there are both religious and secular arguments for more than one point of view. There is no need for believers and non-believers to assemble on opposite sides.

Looking Outwards ...

The view propounded by Darwin and taken up by Peter Singer and others has considerable appeal: progressive development and refinement of moral thinking. It starts by endorsing instinctive, inherited social behaviour (care of the young, acquisition and protection of territory, loyalty to the tribe). Then, as our sympathies, altruistic feelings and intellectual capabilities develop, so we come to care for the wider community, for people in distant lands and for other species.

There is another way in which our moral thinking can expand from the narrow frame to a broader vision. Much of our moral thinking is concerned with avoiding wrongdoing: 'do not kill', 'do not steal', 'do not lie' etc. Moral considerations impose boundaries, which are necessary but unwelcome. Within those boundaries morality has nothing to say, and we do as we please. It is possible to approach some of the issues discussed in sections 3-1 and 3-2 in this way, but there is another kind of moral thinking, characterised by personal integrity and a caring concern for others (the morality of beyond), which pervades our lives to a much greater extent. We welcome moral thinking, and allow it to touch every aspect of our lives. Moral living is not just a matter of avoiding wrongdoing: it is more a matter of setting ideals and doing what we can to live up to them.

...And to the Future

It is a human characteristic to care about what happens after we are dead. The point about Sam Goldwyn's quip, 'What did posterity ever do for me?' is that we know very well that, in caring about the future, our altruistic sense extends beyond the logic of reciprocity. Why do we care? If we do care about the future of our species, should the moral sense be one of the tools that we use to protect it? Should we make an effort to understand the moral sense and nurture it?

More than 99 per cent of all the species that have ever existed on earth are now extinct: extinction, not survival, is the norm. As we look at the world at the beginning of the twenty-first century, we can see several threats to the survival and future well-being of the human species. There is the threat of nuclear, chemical and biological weapons, and there are the threats of environmental damage discussed on page 76. Our inherited instincts and the forces of natural selection, as traditionally understood, with their narrow focus on the ability of an individual to survive and have offspring who inherit the instincts of their parents as well as their physical characteristics, are powerless to protect humanity from these threats: indeed, success in natural-selection terms leads to overpopulation, and this in turn leads to environmental damage and exhaustion of natural resources.

Our moral sense is one of our most valuable possessions. If we care about the future, if we care about human happiness and well-being, if we care about the planet we live on, we will see our moral sense as something to be cherished, not derided, to be nurtured and refined, not ridiculed and brushed aside. If we disapprove of some moral principle or moral code, we should respond with reasoned, moral argument to establish higher moral principles and nobler moral codes, not with a cynical attack on the whole notion of morality. By such reasoned debate, we can hope to establish a morality of consensus, to the benefit of ourselves and future generations.

References

Allison, A C, 1954a. Protection afforded by sickle-cell trait against subtertian malarial infection. *British Medical Journal* (6 Feb 1954), 290–294. Quoted in Ridley (1997).

Allison, A C, 1954b. Notes on sickle-cell polymorphism. *Annals of Human Genetics*, 19, 39–57. Quoted in Ridley (1997).

Austen, Jane, 1816. *Emma*.

Ayer, A J, 1936. *Language, Truth and Logic*. Victor Gollancz. Quoted in Singer (1994).

Blackburn, Simon, 2001. *Being Good*. Oxford: Oxford University Press.

Bronowski, J, 1949. Unbelief and Science. 164–169 in *Ideas and Beliefs of the Victorians*. London: Sylvan Press.

Brosnan, Sarah F, and de Waal, Frans B M, 2003. Monkeys reject unequal pay. *Nature* 425, 297–299.

Brown, Donald E, 1991. *Human Universals*. New York: McGraw-Hill. (List reproduced in Pinker, 2002.)

Chomsky, Noam, 1988. *Language and Problems of Knowledge: the Managua Lectures*. Cambridge, MA: MIT Press. (Quoted by Katz, 2000.)

Clayton, Philip and Schloss, Jeffrey (editors), 2004. *Evolution and Ethics: Human Morality in Biological and Religious Perspective*. Grand Rapids, Michigan / Cambridge, UK: William B Eerdmans Publishing Company

Colby, A, Kohlberg, L, Gibbs, J C and Lieberman, M, 1983. A longitudinal study of moral judgment. *Monographs of the Society for Research in Child Development*, 48.

Connolly, Joseph, 1979. *P G Wodehouse: an illustrated biography*. London: Orbis Publishing.

Cronin, Helena, 1991. *The Ant and the Peacock*. Cambridge: Cambridge University Press.

Dante Alighieri, ca 1320. *The Divine Comedy: 3, Paradise*. (Translated by Dorothy L Sayers and Barbara Reynolds. Harmondsworth: Penguin, 1962.)

Darwall, Stephen (editor), 2003. *Virtue Ethics*. Oxford: Blackwell.

Darwin, Charles, 1872. *The Origin of Species by Means of Natural Selection, or the Preservation of Favoured Races in the Struggle for Life*. Sixth (and final) edition. London: John Murray. (First edition 1859.)

Darwin, Charles, 1874. *The Descent of Man*. Second edition. Republished 1998, New York: Prometheus Books. (First edition 1871.)

Davies, Robert, 1993. *Out of Prison*. Buxton: Church in the Market Place Publications.

Dawkins, Richard, 1976. *The Selfish Gene*. Oxford: Oxford University Press.

Dawkins, Richard, 1986. *The Blind Watchmaker*. Harlow: Longman.

Dennett, Daniel, 1995. *Darwin's Dangerous Idea: Evolution and the Meaning of Life*. New York: Simon and Schuster. (Harmondsworth: Penguin, 1996.)

Dixon, Alan F, 1998. *Primate Sexuality*. Oxford: Oxford University Press.

Dover, Gabriel, 2000a. *Dear Mr Darwin: Letters on the evolution of life and human nature*. London: Orion.

Dover, Gabriel, 2000b. Anti-Dawkins. 47–66 in Rose and Rose (2000).

Ehrlich, Paul R, 2000. *Human Natures*. Washington DC: Island Press / Shearwater Books.

Flack, Jessica C and de Waal, Frans B M, 2000. 'Any animal whatever': Darwinian building blocks of morality in monkeys and apes. 1–29 in Katz (2000).

Foot, P R, 1954. When is a principle a moral principle? *Proceedings of the Aristotelian Society*, Supplementary Volume 28, 95–110.

Frazer, J G, 1922. *The Golden Bough* (abridged edition). London: Macmillan.

Gazzaniga, Michael S, 2005. *The Ethical Brain*. New York: Dana Press.

Gillibrand, Eileen and Mosley, Jenny, 1997. *When I go to work I feel guilty*. London: HarperCollins.

Goddard, Andrew, 2003. *When is War Justified?* Cambridge: Grove Books.

Golding, William, 1954. *Lord of the Flies*. London: Faber.

Goodall, Jane, 1990. *Through a Window*. London: Orion.

Gosling, Samuel D, Kwan, Virginia S Y and John, Oliver P, 2003. A dog's got personality: a cross-species comparative approach to personality judgements in dogs and humans. *Journal of Personality and Social Psychology*, 85, 6, 1161–1169.

Gregory, Richard L (editor), 2004. *The Oxford Companion to the Mind*. Second edition. Oxford: Oxford University Press.

Haarsma, Loren, 2004. Evolution and Divine Revelation: Synergy, Not Conflict, in Understanding Morality. 153–170 in Clayton and Schloss (2004).

Hailsham, Lord, 1994. *Values: Collapse and Cure*. London: HarperCollins.

Hare, R M, 1952. *The Language of Morals*. Oxford: Clarendon Press.

Hare, R M, 1989. *Essays in Moral Theory*. Oxford: Oxford University Press. Quoted in Singer (1994).

Harris, Thomas A, 1967, *I'm OK – You're OK*. (London: Arrow, 1995.)

Hinde, Robert A, 2002. *Why Good is Good: the Sources of Morality*. London: Routledge.

Hirst, Paul H, 1974. *Moral Education in a Secular Society*. London: Hodder and Stoughton, National Children's Home.

Holloway, R, 1999. *Godless Morality*. Edinburgh: Canongate.

Honderich, Ted (editor), 2005. *The Oxford Companion to Philosophy*. Second edition. Oxford: Oxford University Press.

Hume, David, 1739/40. *A Treatise on Human Nature*. Quoted in Singer (1994).

Huxley, Thomas Henry, 1895. *Evolution & Ethics and other Essays*. (Volume IX of Collected Essays.) London: Macmillan.

Jones, Steve, 2000. *The Language of the Genes*. Revised edition. London: Flamingo. (First edition 1993.)

Kant, Immanuel, 1788. *The Critique of Practical Reason*.

Katz, Leonard D (editor), 2000. *Evolutionary Origins of Morality.* Exeter: Imprint Academic.

Kitwood, Tom, 1990. *Concern for Others: A new psychology of conscience and morality.* London: Routledge.

Knight, M, 1955. *Morals without religion and other essays.* London: Dennis Dobson.

Kohlberg, L, 1981. *Essays on Moral Development. Volume 1.The Philosophy of Moral Development.* New York.

Koocher, Gerald P and Keith-Spiegel, Patricia, 1998. *Ethics in Psychology: Professional Standards and Cases.* Second edition. Oxford: Oxford University Press.

Kummer, Hans, 2000. Ways beyond appearances. 48–52 in Katz (2000).

Kuper, Adam and Kuper, Jessica (editors), 1996. *The Social Science Encyclopedia.* Second edition. London: Routledge.

Lahti, David C, 2004. "You Have Heard … but I Tell You …": A test of the Adaptive Significance of Moral Evolution. 132–150 in Clayton and Schloss (2004).

Lewis, C S, 1940. *The Problem of Pain.* London: Geoffrey Bles.

Lewis, C S, 1943. *The Abolition of Man.* Oxford: Oxford University Press.

Lewis, C S, 1952. *Mere Christianity.* London: Geoffrey Bles.

Lewis, C S, 1964. *Letters to Malcolm, chiefly on prayer.* London: Geoffrey Bles.

Lorenz, K, 1952. *King Solomon's Ring.* Translated by Marjorie Kerr Wilson. London: Methuen.

Lorenz, K, 1954. *Man meets Dog.* Translated by Marjorie Kerr Wilson. London: Methuen.

Lorenz, K, 1966. *On Aggression.* Translated by Marjorie Latzke. London: Methuen.

McCall Smith, Alexander, 2004. *The Sunday Philosophy Club.* London: Little, Brown.

McCrum, Robert, 2004. *Wodehouse: a life.* London: Penguin.

McGarvey, Robert, 2005. The ethics of free market capitalism. *Britain & Overseas,* 35, 2, 15–24.

McGinn, Colin, 1979. Evolution, Animals and the Basis of Morality. *Inquiry,* 22, 92–98. Quoted in Singer (1994).

Mackie, J L, 1977. *Ethics: inventing right and wrong.* Harmondsworth: Penguin.

McMichael, M J, 1993. *Planetary Overload.* Cambridge: Cambridge University Press.

Malan, David H, 1995. *Individual Psychotherapy and the Science of Psychodynamics.* Second edition. Oxford: Butterworth-Heinemann.

Masters, Brian, 1996. *The Evil that Men Do.* London: Doubleday.

May, Larry, Friedman, Marilyn and Clark, Andy (editors), 1996. *Mind and Morals: Essays in cognitive science and ethics.* Cambridge, MA: MIT Press.

Midgley, Mary, 1983. Duties concerning Islands. *Encounter,* 60/2, 36–44. Quoted in Singer (1994).

Midgley, Mary, 1991. *Can't we make moral judgements?* New York: St Martin's Press.

Midgley, Mary, 1994. *The Ethical Primate.* London: Routledge.

Midgley, Mary, 1995. *Beast and Man.* Revised edition. London: Routledge. (First edition 1979.)

Midgley, Mary, 2003. *Heart and Mind*. Revised edition. London: Routledge. (First edition 1981.)

Milgram, Stanley, 2004. Obedience, Milgram on. 677–679 in Gregory (2004).

Miller, H, 1857. *The Testimony of the Rocks*. Edinburgh: Thomas Constable & Co, Shepherd & Elliot. (Cambridge: St Matthew Publishing Ltd, 2001.)

Mitchell, Basil, 1969. The historical approach to ethics, especially those of Christianity. 37–43 in Ebling, F J (editor). *Biology and Ethics*. Symposium of the Institute of Biology, No. 18. London: Academic Press (for the Institute of Biology).

Montefiore, H, 1985. *The Probability of God*. London: SCM Press.

Moore, G E, 1903. *Principia Ethica*. Cambridge: Cambridge University Press.

Morgan, Patricia, 2002. *Marriage-Lite: the rise of cohabitation and its consequences*. London: Institute for the Study of Civil Society.

Morgan, Patricia, 2004. Family Structure and Economic Outcomes. *Economic Research Council, Research Study* No. 20.

Murdoch, Iris, 1992. *Metaphysics as a Guide to Morals*. London: Chatto & Windus.

Nagel, Thomas, 1979. *Mortal Questions*. Cambridge: Cambridge University Press.

Nagel, Thomas, 1987. *What does it all mean?* Oxford: Oxford University Press. Quoted in Singer (1994).

Niblett, W R, 1963. Some Problems in Moral Education Today. 13–30 in *Moral Education in a Changing Society*. W R Niblett (editor). London: Faber and Faber.

O'Hear, Anthony, 1997. *Beyond Evolution*. Oxford: Oxford University Press.

O'Hear, Anthony, 1999. *After Progress*. London: Bloomsbury.

O'Neill, Onora, 2002. *A Question of Trust*. BBC Reith Lectures. Cambridge: Cambridge University Press.

Oppenheimer, Helen, 1965. *The Character of Christian Morality*. London: The Faith Press.

Piaget, Jean, 1932. *The Moral Judgment of the Child*. Translated by Marjorie Gabain. London: Routledge and Kegan Paul.

Pinker, Steven, 2002. *The Blank Slate: The Modern Denial of Human Nature*. London: Penguin.

Pope, Alexander, 1733/34. Essay on Man.

Railton, Peter, 2000. Darwinian building blocks. 55–60 in Katz (2000).

de Reuck, A V S, 1969. Discussion. 34–35 in Ebling, F J (editor). *Biology and Ethics*. Symposium of the Institute of Biology, No. 18. London: Academic Press (for the Institute of Biology).

Ridley, Mark (editor), 1997. *Evolution*. Oxford Readers. Oxford: Oxford University Press.

Ridley, Matt, 1993. *The Red Queen*. London: Penguin.

Rogers, Carl R, 1951. *Client-centred Therapy*. London: Constable.

Rolnick, Philip A, 2004. Darwin's Problems, Neo-Darwinian Solutions, and Jesus' Love Commands. 302–317 in Clayton and Schloss (2004).

Rose, Hilary and Rose, Steven (editors), 2000. *Alas, Poor Darwin: Arguments Against Evolutionary Psychology*. London: Random House.

Rose, Steven, 2005. *The 21st Century Brain*. London: Random House.

Ruark, Robert, 1955. *Something of Value*. Hamish Hamilton.

Ruse, M, 1979. *Sociobiology: Sense or Nonsense?* Dordrecht: D Reidel.

Ruse, M, 1991. The significance of evolution. 500–508 in Singer (1991).

Ruse, M and Wilson, E O, 1986. Moral philosophy as applied science. *Philosophy*, 61, 173–192.

Russell, Bertrand, 1930. *The conquest of happiness*. London: George Allen & Unwin.

Russell, Bertrand, 1940. *An Inquiry into Meaning and Truth*. (London: Unwin, 1959, 1980.)

Russell, Bertrand, 1954. *Human Society in Ethics and Politics*. London: Allen and Unwin.

Russell, Bertrand, 1960. Notes on PHILOSOPHY, January 1960. *Philosophy*, 35, 146–147.

Sapolsky, Robert M, 2001. *A Primate's Memoir: Love, Death and Baboons in East Africa*. London: Random House.

Sartre, J P, 1946. Existentialism is a Humanism. In *Existentialism from Dostoevsky to Sartre*, Kaufman, W (Editor). Quoted in Singer (1994).

Scruton, Roger, 1996. *Animal rights and wrongs*. London: Demos.

Sen, Amartya, 1987. *On Ethics and Economics*. Oxford: Blackwell.

Sen, Amartya, 1999. *Development as Freedom*. Oxford: Oxford University Press.

Silberbauer, George, 1991. Ethics in small-scale societies. 14–28 in Singer (1991).

de Silva, Padmasiri, 1991. Buddhist ethics. 58–68 in Singer (1991).

Simpson, Joe, 1988. *Touching the void*. London: Random House.

Singer, Peter, 1981. *The Expanding Circle: Ethics and Sociobiology*. (Oxford: Oxford University Press, 1983.)

Singer, Peter (editor), 1991. *A Companion to Ethics*. Oxford: Blackwell.

Singer, Peter (editor), 1994. *Ethics*. Oxford Readers. Oxford: Oxford University Press.

Smith, Joan, 2001. *Moralities*. London: Penguin.

Sober, Elliott and Wilson, David Sloane, 2000. Summary of *Unto Others: the evolution and psychology of unselfish behaviour*. 185–206 in Katz (2000)

Stenmark, Mikael, 2001. *Scientism: science, ethics and religion*. Aldershot: Ashgate.

Stevens, Anthony and Price, John, 1966. *Evolutionary Psychiatry*. London: Routledge.

Stevens, Anthony, 1998. *An Intelligent Person's Guide to Psychotherapy*. London: Duckworth.

Talbot, Colin, 2005. *The Paradoxical Primate*. Exeter: Imprint Academic.

Tallis, Raymond, 2004. *Why the Mind is not a Computer*. Second edition. Exeter: Imprint Academic.

Taylor, Howard, 2004. *Human Rights: its culture and moral confusions*. Edinburgh: Rutherford House.

Teichman, Jenny and Evans, Katherine C, 1995. *Philosophy: a beginner's guide*. Second edition. Oxford: Blackwell.

Tennyson, Alfred, 1850. *In Memoriam*.

Tinbergen, Niko, 1953. *The Herring Gull's World*. London: Collins.

Tjeltveit, Alan C, 1999. *Ethics and Values in Psychotherapy*. London: Routledge.

Trivers, Robert, 1971. The evolution of reciprocal altruism. *Quarterly Review of Biology*, 46, 35–57. Quoted in Singer (1994).

Troyer, John, 2000. Human and other natures. 62–65 in Katz (2000).

Tutu, Desmond, 1999. *No Future Without Forgiveness*. London: Random House.

Vardy, Peter, 1989. *Business Morality*. London: Marshall Pickering.

Vardy, Peter and Grosch, Paul, 1999. *The Puzzle of Ethics*. Second edition. London: Fount.

Vidler, A R, 1965. Religious Belief Today and its Moral Derivatives. 78–95 in *Moral Education in a Changing Society*. W R Niblett (editor). London: Faber and Faber.

de Waal, Frans, 1982. *Chimpanzee Politics*. London: Jonathan Cape.

de Waal, Frans, 1989. *Peacemaking among Primates*. Cambridge, MA: Harvard University Press.

de Waal, Frans B M, 1996. *Good Natured: the origins of right and wrong in humans and other animals*. Cambridge, MA: Harvard University Press.

de Waal, Frans, 1997. *Bonobo: the forgotten ape*. Berkeley: University of California Press.

de Waal, Frans, 2001. *The Ape and the Sushi Master*. London: Penguin.

Warnock, Mary, 1998. *An Intelligent Person's Guide to Ethics*. London: Duckworth.

Westermarck, E, 1912. *The Origin and Development of the Moral Ideas*, Vol. 1. London: Macmillan. (Quoted by de Waal, 2001.)

Williams, Bernard, 1973. A Critique of Utilitarianism. 96–100, 110–117 in *Utilitarianism for and against*, J J C Smart and Bernard Williams. Cambridge: Cambridge University Press. (Quoted in Singer, 1994.)

Wilson, Edward O, 1975. *Sociobiology: the new synthesis*. Cambridge, MA: Harvard University Press.

Wilson, James Q, 1993. *The Moral Sense*. New York: Free Press.

Wise, Steven M, 2001. *Rattling the Cage*. London: Profile. (First published 1999.)

Wodehouse, P G, 1929. *Summer Lightning*. London: Herbert Jenkins.

Wright, Derek, 1971. *The Psychology of Moral Behaviour*. Harmondsworth: Penguin.

Wright, Robert, 1994. *The Moral Animal*. New York: Pantheon Books. (London: Abacus, 1996.)

Yates, Simon, 1997. *Against the Wall*. London: Jonathan Cape.

Young, Robert, 1991. The implications of determinism. 534–542 in Singer (1991).

Index